HEARTS

On The High School Floor

LEADERSHIP PRINCIPLES TO TRANSFORM A GENERATION

by Cameron & Renee Bennett

Ark House Press
arkhousepress.com

Some names and identifying details have been changed to protect the privacy of individuals.

Cataloguing in Publication Data:
Title: Hearts on the High School Floor
ISBN: 978-1-7643052-2-8 (pbk)
Subjects: [REL109030] RELIGION / Christian Ministry / Youth; [REL091000] RELIGION / Christian Education / Children & Youth; [REL108030] RELIGION / Christian Living / Leadership & Mentoring.

Design by initiateagency.com

Other Books by Cameron and Renee Bennett

A 45 Day Devotional: Break the Rules (Book 1)

A 45 Day Devotional: We the People (Book 2)

To Young People

...our hearts will beat wild and hard for you until the day they beat no more. You are our life's work.

x x x Cam and Renee

TABLE OF CONTENTS

PART 2. TRANSFORMING LEADERS

PART 3. TRANSFORMING YOUTH MINISTRIES

PART 4. TRANSFORMING YOUTH

INTRODUCTION

If you've picked up this book, you must love young people. From the bottom of our hearts, thank you! They need someone just like you. Young people have had our hearts for over 25 years. They are a pretty special bunch for God to have chosen *them* to live through *this* time in history, but God also chose *you* to lead them.

From decades of observation, we have found that young people are hungry not to follow those with the biggest platforms, but the biggest hearts. The ones willing to get themselves elbow deep in the mess of life with them. They want to follow someone they look up to and be transformed in the process.

For us, great influence is not found in following what has worked for someone else, but happens in a unique way, when you discover and outwork God's blueprint for you. We simply share ours to inspire you to find yours. In opening these pages you are glimpsing our heart, which beats hard and wild for the youth.

By the way, you will notice these words are written by me (Renee), but that's only because I'm the writer out of us both. It might be my words but it's our life's work.

Love

Cam and Renee

PART 1
TRANSFORMING YOU

ESSENTIAL 1

You'll never make a difference by being like everyone else

Let's begin at the beginning.

Let's begin where it all began, as we remember it. If this beginning had never taken place, our lives would not be the lives we are living today. This beginning we were a part of, shaped and reshaped youth and youth ministries across our country and beyond.

Just over 20 years ago, youth ministries looked nothing like they do today. The focus was to gather small groups of youth in a home to have fun, play games and share what we called 'supper'. It was nice. Until a man called Russell Evans[1] came along, with a new pattern to build by. It was a pattern never seen before and people were curious, but suspicious and doubtful of his methods. He and a few leaders gathered students in a school hall with no games, no food, no entertainment. Instead, he sat them in a circle, dimmed the lights and strummed his guitar. He

---

[1]   Russell Evans is the founder and senior pastor of Planetshakers Church and Ministry

began to worship, simple songs that were familiar. They sang – softly, tentatively and shyly.

One at a time, a student sat in the middle of the circle and everyone began to encourage them. *God loves you. There's a great plan for your life. We love you being here. You are important to us and to God.* It was simple, yet profound. They spoke purpose and destiny until hearts came undone on that high school auditorium floor. In the dark, with nothing but a guitar, these young people encountered God. By the time parents rolled up in their cars to collect their kids, lights shining into the auditorium windows, all they would see were knees on wooden floors and heads bowed. Unseen hearts were transformed. They came back, week after week, hungry for connection, purpose and a God encounter.

Soon we moved to the church basement. Russell moved between guitar and keyboard, leading, preaching, giving altar calls. When a scruffy, curly haired young guy walked in one day, his left hand swinging a Hungry Jack's bag, God spoke to Russell. *He's your guy. Get him to play.* Russell didn't even know if he could but it turned out that he could. He could play everything, Henry Seely.[2] A team was birthed. I was there, right in the middle, as a miracle unfolded in ways we'd never witnessed before. Hundreds flocked to the meetings. A new pattern of youth ministry in Australia was birthed and all because one man had the vision and the courage to try something that had never been done before.

Growing up we were allowed to wear what we wanted to school. There were no rules and we all lived out our days in a flurry of colour. There were Ford and Holden jackets and jeans with pockets that went to our

---

[2] Henry Seely is Grammy award winning mix engineer / founder of The Belonging Co / Worship leader

knees. Tie dye was the go and even more so if paired with Doc Martin shoes. Rips in jeans didn't mean you'd fallen over and nobody cared that shoulder pads made you look wider, because that was perfectly okay.

No one cared or judged you for what you wore to school. It was just you simply being you.

Then it became compulsory to wear uniforms. We came to school en masse in a sea of pale blue shirts, starched collars, knotted ties and blazers designed to restrict any form of movement. There were rules by the dozen. No make-up, one piece of jewellery allowed, hair cut above the collar, hem lines down to the knees. It was about discipline and conformity.

There's a little resemblance here to youth ministry. We think we have the niche, the point of difference offering up a flurry of colour and styles. But in reality we are getting lost in a sea of uniforms, looking the same, sounding the same. The lights, the games, Instagram. We perform by the unspoken rules of conformity. Be entertaining. Be the coolest, biggest, loudest, the best. To a degree there's nothing wrong with that, and there are certain things that are on trend and we all want to be relevant.

However there is nothing uniform about God. He builds and creates in the most outrageous, outlandish of ways. Lights that twinkle at night in a sky that changes colour as it wills. Animals that slither along the ground and those that fly in the air. A sun that radiates heat and a wind we can feel but not see, clouds that look like cotton wool but cry rain when they become full. God is marvellous and a Master of creativity. He comes to us in a burst of colour, light and sound, but offers us a calm, dark and quiet night.

God's patterns are wild and unconventional, like putting tassels on people's clothes to remind them to be pure (Numbers 15:38-41) and communicating a message through a donkey (Numbers 22:21-35). He asked the prophet Hosea to marry a prostitute (Hosea 1:1-3) and used a star to communicate to some astrologers that Jesus had been born (Matthew 2:1-2).

God doesn't want us to build our youth ministries by the same patterns. Matthew 5 speaks of bringing out the God colours in the world and we can't do that if we are all uniform. God's heart is for light and dark and hues and tints of every variety.

A few years after Russell and Sam, (Russell's wife), moved on from the youth group, it lost its way a little. What God had done in those few years lost momentum and energy. Russell, using his prophetic gift, suggested we, Cameron and I, come on staff to run the youth ministry. This was never part of our plan! We thought our days in youth leadership were long over. I'd given up a full-time teaching job to have Georgia and Cameron was on staff part time overseeing New Christians. We felt compelled to say yes. There was no Instagram, no weekly photographer. We didn't care what others 'out there' were doing. It was simpler back then. We weren't looking for our name in lights, or a preaching gig or any accolades to be bestowed upon us. We loved Jesus. We loved young people. We knew we were called.

There were some very specific patterns we felt God wanted us to build on. One of them was to stop the buses coming from a low socio-economic part of Adelaide. *But God we can't do that. Those kids need us.* However, we felt God was clear on this, so we did. The students that were coming in on those buses were dominating the culture of the youth ministry, but not in a good way. The church kids were no longer coming because of them. So we stopped the buses. We focussed on getting the culture right, bringing the church kids back to youth again and then we would start the buses.

Don't worry about flashy programs, God said. *Just bring My presence back to Solid Rock and I will do the rest.* So we had the next part of our pattern. Everything we did was so young people could encounter Jesus. We taught them what praise was. We set the tone in simple ways to create an atmosphere where young people could encounter Jesus again. We gathered at the altar together. We all stood, didn't allow anyone to sit. We prayed. We prophesied. They cried bucket loads. We loved on them. It was simple, yet it was profound.

A few years later we were overseeing the youth and young adults as Executive Pastors at our church and had become the directors of *Youth Alive South Australia.*[3] *Move to Queensland* God said. *But God, we know everyone here. We have hundreds of friends and family. It's comfortable. Go,* He said. It had never been done before. They couldn't find anyone in Queensland to take over *Youth Alive* and no one had ever left one state to go and run it in another. A leader was always raised up within that state. Yet six months later we packed up the life we knew and drove over the border, strangers in an unfamiliar land.

We could tell you story after story about the ways God has spoken to us about building according to His pattern, not ours and definitely not someone else's. This was nothing like we'd seen on social media or heard about on a website or blog or podcast. God's patterns! Our

---

[3] Youth Alive is a Christian organisation founded by Australian Christian Churches

confidence following Him has strengthened over the years. It's the reason we started a *Youth Alive Conference* when most were adamant that *Youth Alive* don't do conferences. It's why we kept going with *United We Stand*,[4] now the largest youth outreach event in the country, when people didn't understand. It's why we planted a church, from absolutely nothing and kept running *Youth Alive* at the same time. Everyone assumed we would quit, that we couldn't do both. We are now addicted to this life we've been given – this life of living according to God's patterns, not our own. We've seen Him do miracles and we know He will be doing it again in the future.

So we look back and remember the guitars in school halls, stopping the buses, Youth Alive in two states, planting from nothing, gatherings across the country, always confirming that His ways are wild and outlandish.

So go for it. We are here, cheering you on, your biggest supporters. Find the pattern. Build according to the pattern. Be like nobody else you know.

---

[4] United We Stand is a National gathering by Youth Alive, activating young Australians to unite on one night

ESSENTIAL 2

Who you journey with is more important than where you journey too

Leadership should never be done alone. It's a village kind of a thing; living and bleeding together. It's souls intertwining and journeys winding in and around each other like lines on a map. The road is best travelled together. It should sound like the crescendo of an orchestra, the lapping of multiple waves crashing onto the shore. It's not a solo affair. It can't be. Tables, lounges, or bench seats were never made for one.

Our sweetest moments have always been with people right next to us because we have never built anything on our own. Even in the most difficult of times, when you are being pulled underwater and can't catch your breath, you need a hand to hold, someone to pull you up and remind you to breathe. You've got this!

But this kind of friendship doesn't happen overnight. It happens slowly; sneaks up on you in the most pleasant of ways.

When I was a young leader, I found I had been redefined. I had been a child with not many friends. I only ever had one at a time, as if friends could only come in single file. If my friend was away from school, I'd play alone. I'd hide in the alcove so the teacher couldn't see me and feel sorry for me. I hated those days. I grew up believing what my mother told me, *you are like me dear, you don't make friends very easily*.

When I became a youth leader I found I had friends. Not in single file but a big, glorious group of them. These people became my tribe. They wanted to be with me and I loved them dearly for it. We lived life together, often and hard. Discipleship was held at Russell and Sam's house where we belly laughed and cried all within a few hours, until our insides ached but we always left feeling lighter. We ran connect groups together and alongside each other. We were fiercely competitive, all wanting the biggest and to be the best. We gathered youth from our connect groups and took them out as one big group – beach trips, Macca's until midnight, video nights at my house, pool parties at another. We hung together after youth, after church and any other time we could, just because. We jumped into one another's cars and drove for hours that seemed like minutes as we chatted along the way.

We fell in love but sometimes we wouldn't be loved back. There were tensions like that. But at the bottom of it all, we were the best of friends, fiercely loyal to each other. We served God together. There are NO better friendships than those formed when you serve God together. Ministry seems to have a magical kind of glue. We worshipped side by side. We watched miracles unfold right in front of us like the conference that began with us but went on to be the biggest Australian youth had seen, known as Planetshakers. We watched one another's dreams become reality. Music was written. Albums were made. Lives were changed and the years flew by.

However, life is not always sparkly balloons and fairy floss moments. My best friend in those years was a unique and wonderful creature named Bernie. She was hysterical and loved God with all her heart. We shared a cabin at every youth camp we went to. She made up words that I couldn't even spell if I tried. Margherita was not a pizza but her way of saying 'oh my goodness'. She drove like a woman possessed in her dark maroon Toyota, my fingers are still imprinted on her dash. I remember the time we both drove our cars to the beach, filled with youth from our life groups. She tore down Anzac Highway, music blaring until the police pulled in behind her and told her over their loudspeaker to turn the music down. Of course that made us laugh hysterically the rest of the way. She was crazy and wonderful; one of a kind and everyone loved her.

Years rolled by. We grew up together; became real deal adults. We got married and bought houses. We invited one another over for dinner like we were playing families, only this time it was for real. I had a baby. Then another one. While I was pregnant with my second, Bernie got pregnant with her first.

Life got busy for us both, so it became longer between catch ups. But I remember ringing her a few days before she was due to give birth. She was scared. We chatted and I encouraged her. Then she got pre-eclampsia so they delivered her baby early, a beautiful, but tiny, red-headed girl. However, within 24 hours of her giving birth, Bernie suffered a massive bleed to her brain. It was a code blue situation and I got the call within hours. *Pray! Please pray!* They transferred her to intensive care at the Royal Adelaide Hospital. We gathered around her bed together, friends who had fought in the leadership trenches together for so long, chatting with her, laughing, reminding her of days gone by. We pleaded with her about all the days to come. *Come back to us. You have so much more to do.* The silence was ominous!

After a few weeks the machines were turned off and one by one we got *that* call. Her parents' hearts broke as they went home, elated joy mixed with immeasurable sorrow as they brought their grand-daughter home but had to leave their daughter behind. Her husband, devastated, empty and sorrow-filled, drove home from the hospital alone.

I share this with you because sorrow is a part of ministry life too. I shared at Bernie's funeral from Psalms, that one day in the house of the Lord is better than a thousand in the courts of the wicked. It is worth it. To be serving God together is a privilege. I know Bernie thought so and right there, in the church, mourning with hundreds of others, we all knew it. It's worth it, living your life for Jesus and doing it with best friends beside you. I pray you have crazy beach drives and late night Macca's runs; conversations that break you open and put you back together; memories so beautiful that they'll last a lifetime.

So don't give up. On the less than easy days, grit your teeth and take a look around you. Look at the beautiful souls on this journey with you. Hold them a little tighter to you. They truly are God's gift for this life we have chosen.

And Bernie, you are never forgotten, my forever friend. You are imprinted on our hearts for eternity. I can't wait to see you again!

ESSENTIAL 3

Never let anybody make you feel unimportant

Years ago I had a really good friend, you know the kind you consider the real deal; more like family. The kind you can wear no make-up in front of and your worst pair of pyjamas and she won't judge you. We house-sat together. We did ministry together. We laughed until our bellies ached and knew each other's secrets. We did everything together. But niggling a little bit below the surface, like tiny fish darting around your feet in shallow ocean water, I caught quick glimpses of something that made me uncomfortable. I had a quiet suspicion that she often acted superior.

She would never say it aloud but it was whispered in small ways. Like the way she was always a step ahead while I obediently trailed behind. Or her friendly slap on my shoulder and a merry 'you're so cute' that somehow didn't seem like a compliment, but more like a box she had put me in. She even preached about me once, in front of my face. Seriously, I was in the front row. She preached her heart out and even cried about this friend who had hurt her and how God was teaching her things. I shook my head and wondered who could do that to my dear friend. It turned out it was me and I had no clue. What I had supposedly said was never said by me. But regardless, I remember thinking what kind of friend does that – preaches in front of you about you? But I am the forgiving type. I make allowances and bury my hurt.

We were friends for a long time but it always felt a little off, like unbalanced scales; a bit lopsided. I was 'so fortunate' to be one of her friends as though she was the more worthy one. I didn't think for a second that she was lucky to be mine. Eventually life moved us apart. I'd always thought having history with people tied you together in a strong way. Your history is comfortable and comforting. You know things about one another like how your face looked the day you got married and the cute way you waddled when you were pregnant with your first child. I thought these things were like some sort of insurance for a lifelong friendship.

After a while, my friend moved away and she became one of those celebrity Christians that everyone wanted to be around. Her Instagram followers climbed. I was so proud of her. Then one day it dawned on me that she had defriended me. You know when someone only follows 96 people but they have 90k following back. That means you've hit some kind of jackpot, right? Like 'I've made it in life' kind of stuff. I knew that the 96 people she followed must have also been very important people. Apparently I wasn't one of them. My friend, my 'we grew up together' friend, had dropped me just like that.

I admit anger raged in my heart, fierce clouds pushed about in a storm of disbelief. Rejection rose to the surface and bubbled out on my tongue. How dare she? Who does she think she is? But mostly I was hurt because I had allowed it to stick. I must be a 'not important' person. I felt small and insignificant. I would never do that to my friend. It's just not who I am. But behaviour like this gets duly rewarded, right? Nope! Her fame kept rising. Her importance went up. She was on the 'I've made it' speaking circuit. She posted about herself all the time. People clapped and gave her standing ovations with likes and comments.

I just couldn't get over how unkind it was, how unfair it seemed. Sometimes it feels like all the wrong things get rewarded in this world, even in Christian circles. I'm not a self-promoter. I wouldn't ditch a childhood friend if I became 'more important' than them.

I'm not pining for stages and accolades but I don't want to feel unimportant either, like what I'm doing doesn't matter. So I considered becoming 'not me' for a while. I thought maybe I'd start putting up pictures of myself preaching and letting everyone know the platforms I get to be on. I'd unfollow most people on my social media so the ratio of followers to following is like 500 to 1. I wrestled on the inside with the unfairness of it all. But it made me think about you.

Some would say Cameron and I had 'made it', whatever that means, in our position as *Youth Alive Directors*. You might compare yourself to us and that makes you feel unimportant. But that makes my heart very, very sad.

So I opened my Bible and poured my heart out to God telling Him about it all and how I felt. I stumbled across a beautiful phrase; just a little sentence. It was and still is medicine for my soul, the words by which I am determined to live and I hope you will too. The words were written by the Apostle Paul in Romans chapter 4. *'The story we're given is a God-story, not an Abraham story.'*[5]

These words grounded me, brought me back to centre. Made my world right again. Let these words be the foundation by which you live. Phew! It's not about me – remember? It's not about you – remember? We have not been given a Reneè story. We've not been given a (enter your name) story. This is a God story being outworked in and through you. This is the value upon which we must build our lives.

I will do and keep on doing whatever God has purposed for me. I will do it for 10 and I will do it for 1000. I will do it in my sneakers and trackies and when nobody sees. I will do it if it means a microphone and platform. I will do it if it means I'm praying over one or laying hands on many. I will do it even if nobody knows my name, or if I'm not an 'important person' on someone's following list. I'll do it whether people are watching on Instagram or not. I'll even do it when my heart is sad because my friend turned out to be a not-so-good friend. Because this life, my life is about being a part of God's story. It's about all the lives God writes into this story, for me to help. I am not the title of the book. I am not the hero of the story.

Please don't feel like what you are doing in your corner of the world doesn't matter. It does! It matters very much. It matters to that young person who looks up to you like you are their world. It matters to the leaders who you give a place to belong. But most of all, if you are weaving your way through a chapter of God's story, then it matters to Him. Don't trip yourself up on the world's traps by living according to its patterns. God is in charge of your life and your story, not a marketing

---

[5] Full text can be found in Romans 4:1-6 (The Message)

or self-promotion scheme or a social media account. Not the approval of other people or that friend, who turned out to be not a friend at all. We have to let go and let people live their own lives. We are responsible only for ours. If God has anointed us for a task then He will make a way. He alone goes before us and makes crooked paths straight. The story is God's. We are honoured to be a part of it.

Whether the world recognises it or never knows who you are, be encouraged today. You are doing a marvellous job and God is very proud of you.

ESSENTIAL 4

The gift of needing more

Over the years we have sat through hundreds, probably thousands of offering messages. They've challenged us, raised our faith levels and pushed us out of our comfort zone when it comes to our personal giving. We believe with all our heart that God wants us to prosper in our finances, just like He wants us to prosper in our health and our relationships and in our souls.

We are each on our own journey with the above and our finances are no different. If you are a youth pastor or leader, but your bank account is a little on the light side and you tussle with faith around your finances, that's okay!

We're going to go against the grain and be a little counter cultural for a minute. We're suggesting that it's actually a good thing to have to work for things, not be handed everything and to realise that having little resources can actually turn out to be a gift. We love our three kids very much and because we love them, we don't give them everything they want. We are teaching them to work for things, look after what they have and be good stewards with little. We want them to have part-time jobs and buy their own car. We would not be doing them any favours if we handed them whatever they want, whenever they want it.

We have always served God with all our hearts, given our very life and all we have and yet still been rummaging through the console of the car hoping to find enough coins to buy bread and milk. We have been running meetings where God is powerfully moving and touching young people, then driven home to a house where we couldn't afford to concrete the driveway. We've worn clothes from *Cotton On* and hunted for bargains from *Best for Less* to clothe Georgia. We were seeing miracles break out as *Planetshakers*[6] was blowing up and attracting thousands, while back at home our credit card was sitting in a block of ice in the freezer so we couldn't use it and put ourselves in debt.

Did we lack faith? No way. Were we not giving? Absolutely not! We had times when we gave a whole week's wage. But we learnt things that cannot be learned when you have plenty. We learned to steward well with what we had. We learned to be faithful with the little because these things matter to God. We learned to work hard for everything, because when we build things with sweat and toil, it builds character. Who wants to give resources to someone who is merely going to squander it? If we can be careful and responsible and faithful with our portion, then we will be the same with God's. That is such an important lesson to learn and apply to our lives.

When *Planetshakers* was in Adelaide, Cameron was in charge of catering for 1000 people for a week. He was given a strict budget. Not only did

---

[6] Planetshakers is an Australian church and movement known for its music, college, conferences and more

he keep within budget, but through creativity, careful strategizing and smart negotiations with food companies, he was not only able to feed everyone with great food but he actually made money in the process that could be sewn back into the conference.

Every time we ran a youth camp, conference or event, we kept prices down for the young people without ever causing the youth ministry to go into debt. We've seen many youth pastors over the years not able to steward resources well and the church has needed to bail them out. God watches these little things. He is interested in the detail and the integrity we show. Those times we froze our credit card, scraped coins together and tip-toed over mud to get to our front door were hard times and we wondered where our blessing was and when the breakthrough was coming.

Of course we would have liked to have the label clothing, nice shoes and a fancy house. We wanted the new car and the big bank balance. But we have to keep the main game in focus. Don't get swept up in the tidal wave of bigger and better. Peter and John had it right when they told the beggar (paraphrased from Acts 3:6), *silver and gold have we none but what we have we give freely to you in the name of Jesus rise up and walk.*

When we first moved to Queensland, we were told *Youth Alive* was a full-time position. A few weeks after moving our entire family and booking the kids into a private school, everything went belly up. Two weeks after arriving, we found out a regional tour through Queensland had caused a budget deficit of over $100,000. *Youth Alive* was handed to us with that debt. Our full-time job turned into half-time. It was too late to back out and go home. But we had learned to be faithful with little. We knew how to work hard. We had made money from catering budgets, never lost money on camps and events. We could shop at *Jay Jays* when we had to! Having done much with little turned out to be a gift that served us well in that season. Within 18 months, Cameron had brought *Youth Alive* completely out of debt! It has never been in debt since.

A few years ago we started a church from nothing. We borrowed no money from anywhere. We had 11 people in our lounge-room and a great deal of faith. While other church plants have budgets of hundreds of thousands, we didn't ask for one cent. *Public*[7] is well on the way to being a thriving community and no resources have been wasted or squandered. God can trust us when we live like that.

None of this has come from being given large sums of money. It's come from being faithful and careful with the little we have. It's about doing the boring stuff, the non-glamorous, like budgeting. It's about being responsible and not going to Mum and Dad or our Senior Pastor to bail us out. Why would God give us a bigger budget in the future when we can't steward the money that's not ours now?

When we are faithful with little, God's word says He can trust us with much. What was a small catering budget over 20 years ago, has become a massive budget now we run *Youth Alive*. It takes a mix of faith and character and a whole lot of integrity to steward the little and work hard.

---

[7] Public is a church in Queensland, Australia, founded by Cameron and Renee Bennett

ESSENTIAL 5

It's okay not to be okay

The rabbit hole – it's the deep, dark place that we go down when we are not okay. I know what it's like to feel like you're falling down the rabbit hole, because I've fallen down there myself, on more than one occasion. It can be a dark place of anxiety or depression, the abyss where we find all sorts of secret fears and addictions. I know how dark and scary it is, to look up and not be able to see the light, to feel stuck, afraid and helpless, worrying that nobody knows you are there so any hope of rescue is impossible. To jump and claw, and try and climb out by yourself, only to feel your body slide back down that slippery slope, exhausted, frightened, a hopeless mess at the bottom.

Let my words be an anchor for you today, a rope thrown down to your hands. In that dark place, grab on to them and hold on for dear life. Let them remind you that someone knows you are there and you won't always feel quite as bad. There is a way out of the rabbit hole.

I slid down a few years ago. It was a panic attack in the middle of an *Aldi Supermarket.* My shopping was piled high on the conveyor belt and right there, surrounded by peanut butter, bags of apples and laundry detergent, an old man behind me and the check out lady in front, my heart began to pound. My vision was peppered with stars, my hands were clammy and my breath caught in my throat. I had visions of passing out, an ambulance coming and waking up, embarrassed by all the commotion I'd caused. Silly ol' me! After a few minutes, my world became right side up again. I quickly packed my bags and rushed out to the car. *What just happened? Maybe I have a virus*, I thought. But a few weeks later I knew it wasn't a virus when it happened again. This time while sipping coffee, relaxed and slow at my favourite cafe. My suspicions became confirmation I was having panic attacks. Anxiety had gripped me. I was falling down the rabbit hole – again.

I was so embarrassed I didn't want anyone to know I was there. I hid it, ashamed. *This isn't me. I'm capable and strong. I'm a pastor. I help others.* I couldn't get up on a stage to preach. *What if I had another episode?* Lining up in shopping lanes became my greatest fear. I wore sunglasses, as a sort of protective shield from my irrational fears.

I know how you feel. I see you. I am you. Now that I have climbed out of that rabbit hole, although standing on wobbly knees at the top, I am leaning over the side to call out to you. Listen! Turn your ears and heart my way. It's going to be okay. You are going to be okay. But for now, it's okay to not be okay.

There are so many of us these days. We are used to being fixers and healers, yet we find ourselves in a place of needing fixing and healing for ourselves and there are far more of us than we realise.

One of the best things I discovered during that time was my 'person'. Find your person. Mine was Cameron. I let him in, tried to find the words so he could 'find' me. The act of being able to tell someone, to let him in even though he'd never been there himself, brought comfort. I'd tell him about my worst moments without fear of being judged. Just hearing the words *it's ok* and *you won't always feel this way* brought a glimmer of light into that otherwise dark place.

Perhaps the greatest thing I learned was not to try to fix it myself. It's better if you don't try and get better, because the pressure of trying to feel better and be better, often sends us right back to the place we are trying to get out of. It adds weight and stress, which makes it worse. The desperate 'trying' to fix myself with Scriptures and worship, books and relaxation time, only made me feel worse.

Healing came with acceptance. It came with gratefulness. I had to get to the point where I was truly grateful this challenge had come into my life. Grateful because it came to teach me something, show me something about myself, the way I lived and processed life. I began to see it as a beautiful friend, truly welcome in my life. As crazy as that sounds, it was the very act of acceptance that short-circuited the fear. Allowing the darkness to be present instead of frantically trying to push it away, brought me sweet relief. I came to the place where I was ok sitting in the rabbit hole. I was ok with being there and gave myself permission to sit in the dark. I gathered the courage to whisper into it *what have you come to show me?*

Perhaps the greatest gift of all is that you, better than anybody else, will understand what the young people in your care are going through. It is unfortunately a pandemic of this generation.

A few pages are not going to change your life, but if in reading these words you feel a little comfort, know that there is no shame in falling down the rabbit hole and don't be afraid to sit there for a while. Even the darkest night will eventually give way to the light of a new day.

ESSENTIAL 6

Our roots are revealed in our fruit

We are human and we hurt. To be alive is to sometimes be wounded. It's what makes us broken and beautiful, all at once. Our scars set us apart and make us who we are. They are a reminder that we are stronger than whatever tried to break us.

We cannot take people beyond where we have gone ourselves, therefore most leadership is actually about honesty, digging deep and facing our most hidden parts. God will place His finger on areas of our life that will rise to the surface again and again until we give in and deal with them. We all have stuff to deal with but we can choose whether these things remain secrets in the dark and grow in their power over us, or whether they will be defeated and we will grow through the experience.

The strength of a tree depends on the health of its root system. Our health as a person and a leader depends on what is going on deep down in our heart. Even when we think we have gotten away with hiding it from the world, it will show up in the fruit we produce, for fruit can only be as healthy as the tree that produced it.

What makes an extraordinary leader is someone who leads from the heart. It is not talent, ability or how cool we are. It's not our program or the way we hype the crowd. It's what we carry inside of us. It's our ability to face ourselves honestly and with vulnerability. It's to know it's more than okay to have some broken places, because that's where God can make His home and go to work in us.

It's not about being perfect but being perfectly aware of what's going on at a deeper level. It's about not keeping secrets but opening our hearts and fully exploring who we really are. It's working out the patterns of our behaviour and knowing our weak spots, the parts that bruise easily.

We've been in this game long enough to watch people's journey. There have been those who have had a glorious rise in the world of leadership and ministry and then had equally spectacular falls. People love watching the rise but when somebody ends up sprawled flat on the ground, it scares us and so we tip-toe away, not wanting to look. Usually we will mutter something like how could this be and how did that happen. But it is no surprise when what's on the inside doesn't match up with what's being portrayed on the outside. The danger with being on a pedestal is that we feel incredible pressure to hide flaws we think might bring us down. So we push stuff away, disowning it and in the process we are disowning a part of ourselves.

One thing we know to be true is that what lies below has a way of bubbling up to the surface and usually at the most inconvenient of times. The ones who end up falling haven't dealt with themselves honestly. They haven't learned to embrace their vulnerability. They didn't see or did not want to see the root that leads to the downward spiral. Time and pride get in the way and it seems too late. But it's never too late.

God has a habit of taking the broken places and making them into something new and beautiful. What we consider cracks and imperfections are actually places where His light can be seen. He builds a home out of our broken pieces. That home becomes a shelter and comfort to others who, just like we once were, are wandering in the dark alone. If we can be brave enough to allow God and somebody else we trust, to stick their hands inside and touch the core of our pain, then we will know how to do the same for somebody else. We have a whole generation of young people just waiting for somebody who knows how.

ESSENTIAL 7

Ask questions

It's the mantra we live by – always have, always will. There should never be a point in our lives where we think 'we've made it'. We should always be hungry to learn more, always growing. It's not just in leadership but in every area of our lives. When we became parents, we went to our friends Sam and Franca and asked lots of questions. The questions were important. We didn't just ask where did you buy your pram or should we demand feed or do routine? We asked about deeper things. How do we raise a little girl who will be kind? How do we manage three little ones and not get out of the habit of being at church? How do we disciple the moral heart of our kids? They were life changing questions.

Since that has been a pattern in our life, we have been surprised to learn that asking questions doesn't come naturally to most people. We've seen over and over that the best people ask a lot of questions. Some people not only don't know what kind of questions to ask, but they don't think they need to ask any at all. A few years ago, we were asked to catch up with a couple. They were youth leaders that needed a little mentoring.

We are always keen to help anyone so we agreed with enthusiasm. We chatted over mugs of steaming coffee, laughing and catching up. The conversation bounced along nicely until we suggested we catch up regularly, offering to give them any advice, mentoring or help.

We were met with blank, almost cold stares. *Oh we don't need that,* she said. *We have people to go to already,* he said. We asked who these people were and discovered it was a couple of friends, peers, people who were no further along in life than they were. The clincher came next – *we like to be careful who we talk to.*

We almost choked on our coffee. We didn't know whether to feel horrified or rejected. It's not like we were randoms or 'just anyone' who hadn't done anything in life. At this stage we were *National Youth Alive Directors* and had built many healthy, thriving ministries.

But then there are people like Sam and Hannah, a young couple who ran *Youth Alive* in South Australia, our old stomping ground. Sam and Hannah are sponges, soaking in and slurping up everything they can get from us. They ask questions, big life questions. They watch. They've seen what works and they imitate and build on what they have learned. They asked heart questions about marriage and raising babies who love Jesus. When Sam was asked to go and preach in a significant church in the country, it clashed with a regional leadership event in his own state. He was conflicted in his heart. *What should I do?* He called Cameron. Most people would have taken the significant preaching gig in a heartbeat, without a second thought. Sam wrestled with it in his soul so he presented his dilemma to us and we confirmed what he already knew. Preaching gigs would come again, but your own people have to come first.

Is it any wonder Sam and Hannah are growing in leaps and bounds? They grew a youth ministry in regional South Australia to a size that has never been seen before in that region. *Youth Alive* thrived under their leadership.

Asking questions is an art that will serve you well. It will separate you from others. Find people who do life well. Watch them. Ask questions that draw out the gold from the depths of their wisdom and apply it to your life. Never think you know it all, or know better. There is always something to be learned. Ask deep, soul searching questions. The kind that will open people's hearts causing them to sift through and offer you their life earned wisdom.

ESSENTIAL 8

Choosing good or God

The most discussed question amongst youth leaders would have to be *'do you believe in 'the one'?'* They know my answer – I do believe in 'the one' and love at first sight and fairy tales and happily ever afters. I also believe that who you choose to step out in life with is the single most important life-changing decision you will ever make.

I sometimes think that maybe I shouldn't though. There have been more divorces and sad endings in my family than Cinderella could poke her stick at. I've seen the words *'I do'* crumple into a mess of *'I no longer do'* and *'please leave'* too many times to count. I grew up with cousins going through broken homes simultaneously. I was too nervous to believe in love, wasn't sure what to look for and didn't trust in it anyway.

However, when Jesus came into my life, He did something in me. He restored my hope by giving me people to observe how it should be done, like Sam and Russell. Their love for one another was so strong its healing balm spilled out onto me. I watched, because I was hungry to believe that real love actually existed. I found it there, sitting in their green leather lounge. They would sometimes get a bit annoyed with each other and I'd hold my breath. *This must be it. He won't return this time.* But he did. Sometimes they fought, but it never broke them apart. I needed to see that. I needed to see how real love worked because I had only seen it after it was too broken and the damage done.

My belief in true love was restored. I decided I would wait for 'the one' – 'my one'. Other people may have their own theories on this but I can't go past God's absurd promise to Abraham.

God said that he and his wife Sarah would conceive a child. Both in their nineties and having found Sarah was barren they took action and tried to make it happen with Haggai (Sarah's maid) and Ishmael was the result of that union. But he wasn't the promised one. Good try, Abraham, but you got this one wrong, buddy. The promise, the future, the destiny, could only be fulfilled between Abraham and Sarah, the perfect mix, the chosen couple to give birth to a son, who would be named Isaac. Abraham and Sarah would have done better to have trusted in God's plan for them in the first place. That's why I decided to wait for my one. God's choice for me.

Knowing the price paid of broken love and marriages, it makes me sad to see people compromise. They might marry a seemingly good person, but is it God's plan? Every Christmas, my family would question me – *haven't you got a boyfriend YET?* One day, a beautiful teaching colleague of mine, came to my side after the other teachers were heckling me, and said, '*I know what you're waiting for. Keep strong.*'

Thank you, I needed to hear those words that day. I needed someone else to see what I could see and to tell me to be strong and wait, not compromise. So I did. I dated some guys but they left a kind of prickly feeling inside, one that was sharp and rough around the edges. I couldn't tell you the reasons they felt wrong, I just knew they didn't feel right. Right was the elusive thing I was waiting for. I couldn't tell you what it looked like but I could tell you when I didn't see it.

Then there was Cameron. At first, I was scared to let him in and risk having my heart shattered into a thousand pieces. It had happened once before, the day my Dad left. But this time it felt different. I had a peace in my gut and I cautiously proceeded. I fell in slow motion, into a life-long love with this man. This man who is better than good; he was God's plan for me. I desperately wanted my life to count in a spectacular way for Jesus and I knew that Cameron was to be a part of this. So when the day came and I stood at the altar to say 'I do', I did it with all of my heart. I remember almost choking on the words 'til death do us part' because truth be known, I will love Cameron with my whole being even after death has parted us. He tells me at least once a day how much he loves me. He phones me all the time. Twenty seven years feels like just a moment. I could live a lifetime with him and I'm sure it would not be enough.

Perhaps that sounds greedy, but to have grown up and witnessed so much love broken, it has fascinated me watching it blossom and thrive in my own life. The best thing of all was that we were convinced the day we stood at the altar that God had brought us together. Russell said that day that this moment was planned before the beginning of time and I'm sure I heard the angels cheering as we said 'I do'. We absolutely love serving God together. Our hearts beat in time to our God Call. It's interwoven into the fabric of who we are. It's not one trying to keep up with the other or one pulling the other along. We belong together. God put us together. We are night and day, shade and light, but we are perfect together. I pray the same for you. Wait for it. Don't compromise because, when it's right it's extraordinary.

Besides, in the words of Ryan Gosling, aka Noah in the 2004 movie *The Notebook*, *'every day we are together is the greatest day of my life'*. It takes my breath away that God has gifted me with a love like this.

ESSENTIAL 9

Rinse your cottage cheese

Anybody who has been through the *Youth Alive Academy*[8] knows what this means. It has become our mantra, our greatest value, a war cry our students live by. Rinse your cottage cheese.

In his book *Good to Great*,[9] author Jim Collins tells the story of a marathon runner so committed to his goal of achieving his best that he put himself through a strict eating and training plan. In cutting all fat from his diet, he decided to even rinse his cottage cheese, which is already known for having the lowest fat content. He was willing to go to extreme lengths, above and beyond, pushing boundaries to achieve his goals.

---

[8] *Youth Alive Academy is the training Bible college of Youth Alive*
[9] *2001,Good to Great, written by Jim Collins, available from www.randomhouse. co.uk – or email businessbooks@randomhouse.co.uk*

These are the kind of people we want to surround ourselves with. The 'cottage cheese rinsers' are the ones we want on our staff, our youth team and they are what we train our Academy students to be.

What does it look like to rinse your cottage cheese? It looks like excellence, yet not perfection. It looks like extraordinary when others settle for ordinary. It looks like going the extra mile when everyone else can't be bothered. It's picking up that piece of rubbish that others walk over and picking up that kid so they don't miss out on a chance to meet God. It's going to the prayer meeting even when you'd rather watch Netflix and opening your Bible when you'd rather fall asleep. It's watching your online lectures at college though nobody will know if you don't. It's reading the book and highlighting sections instead of skimming. It's doing the most when you could get away with the least.

Poppy rinses her cottage cheese. She keeps turning up in kids' lives, calling them, visiting them, travelling hundreds of kilometres even when she can hardly afford the petrol. She's the first to pick up the broom at church and start the packing up after youth. She rolls the chords and opens the curtains. When Poppy smiles she lights up a room. She does rather than complains. She sees all the things others walk past, the little and the big. She turns up early even when others have stopped doing so months ago. She's creative and sassy and kind. She's your girl-to-get-things-done. We think God looks down from heaven and says, *'I'll take her.'* Not because she's the most talented, even though she has oodles of talent. Not because she has charisma, although she has plenty of that too. But because she *rinses her cottage cheese.* She gives when others have stopped. She turns up when others don't. She does the menial tasks with a smile. She does the small and the unseen, the not so glamorous stuff. She is changing lives because of it. Beautiful, sassy, blonde-haired Poppy!

Give us a whole team of Poppy's, because these *cottage cheese rinsers* are the true world-changers.

ESSENTIAL 10

Honour those who have gone before

What does one do if a blueprint, a vision, has been handed down from the previous leader? It's their baby, precious and invested into with their own hands and time. They've passed it to you tentatively, with great care and clear instructions to take care of it. Then you unroll their blueprint, as original and magnificent as it was, your breath catches because you know that was for then. But this is now.

We've seen this before and experienced it ourselves. However, the very worst thing you can do is crumple it up right before their eyes and with the best of intentions, tell them thank you very much but it's a new day. I've got new ideas. I'm the new breed. Watch this space, I'm coming through.

This type of person picks faults from the season before and now they are going to be the saviour of this ministry.

The leaders who went before us deserve our highest esteem and honour. Even if the blueprint is no longer relevant today, we should be thankful for what they built yesterday. We walk where we do today because of those who laid the path before us. It's no skin off our nose to esteem them and let others know we are thankful too. It actually builds a solid platform of trust. Think of it like this. What about when your time is done and the blueprint you have created is handed to a sassy little punk who sniggers in your face and tosses it out with the trash? No matter what you agree or disagree with about what you have been handed, whether it is a youth group, a connect group, a music team or whatever else, somebody paid a price before you. It deserves our respect.

We ran *Youth Alive in South Australia* for four years before moving to Queensland and taking over there. A few years later we became the National Leaders. This is how we see it. *Youth Alive* has been running for 40 years and we are honoured to have been carrying it for 13 of these. *Youth Alive* existed for decades before us and will go on for decades after us. We are only the caretakers for this season. We are not the owners; it's been placed into our hands to carry for a while. We take this seriously. We are not building for us, or for now, we are building for young people and for generations to come.

After our first few years in Queensland, the amazing blueprint that had always been used previously, started to fail us. It was always the plan to run large scale, evangelistic events in every state around Australia. We would bring in a popular band usually from America, share the costs among all the States and have a good evangelistic preacher take the night out with a punchy salvation message. Hundreds and thousands of young people had been saved this way for decades, but for some reason it had stopped working. Youth ministries have become so good at running their own evangelistic events, they didn't really need us anymore. Our stadiums were filling less while our budgets blew out more. It was no longer a sustainable model. So we went back to the blueprint, the decades old, fail proof blueprint. We unrolled it, examined it and wondered, is it time to write a new one? We felt that yes, it was time.

We could pack up our suitcases and our kids and go back to Adelaide, or we could go back to the drawing board and create a fresh blueprint. So that's what we did. God spoke to us clearly about birthing a youth conference in Queensland. *But what are you doing?* people asked. *Youth Alive doesn't do conferences. That's a silly idea.* We did it anyway.

Then one day, while reading an Australian history book on our Federation, God gave Cameron the crazy idea of bringing evangelism back to grass roots, local level. *United We Stand* was born as he poured over that history book. We decided to run smaller, local events, all at the same time, all throughout Queensland, on the same night. *What do you mean?* people asked. *We don't understand.*

As this was unfolding, we were invited on a trip to *Soul Survivor*[10] in the UK, by our good friend Mike Pilavachi. It's the largest youth conference in Europe, attracting over 30,000 youth and young adults over the course of a month. The night we arrived the meeting had already started. We were taken down to the stage area, which was really just a pit for the muso's to sit when they weren't on stage. There was no VIP front row or special guest area. We immediately loved it. During worship, Mike pulled us onto the stage (slightly awkward moment) and whispered in our ear, *look at this and dream.* We had been handed a gift, right there on the stage, surrounded by 10,000 young people

---

[10] *Soul Survivor UK was a festival that ran from 1993 to 2019, gathering tens of thousands of young people every year to worship Jesus*

singing their hearts out to Jesus. He handed us permission to dream a new dream. *Look at what God is doing here,* he said. *God can do this and more back in Australia.*

Later that week we went for lunch with Mike and over a huge plate of fish and chips and a big mug of apple cider, he filled us with words we will never forget. He said that *Youth Alive* was like a big, beautiful cathedral. It had been worked on by amazing people for decades. It was magnificent and admired and everyone was used to it this way. But we knew that on the inside of this beautifully architected piece of history, the walls were starting to crumble. We were the ones holding it together but we knew its day was done. As wonderful as this cathedral had been, we knew this was not the future.

So we had started to build something that looked a little different. But at that moment all there was were some foundations, raw and ugly and a little under-whelming. A little conference, a few grass roots local outreach events. People didn't/couldn't or wouldn't understand. They questioned us and wondered why our focus was over there, on those foundations, when we had this beautiful cathedral that had stood solid for decades. *But it will be okay,* Mike reassured us. *People will see in time. So be courageous and let go of the cathedral walls and start building what God would want.*

So we came home from that trip and allowed ourselves to leave the cathedral that was and gave ourselves permission to build the foundations that would create what was to be. Hindsight is a very beautiful thing, because those foundations have turned into something else quite magnificent.

A conference that started with 300 people in Queensland is now gathering thousands of youth and young adults in every state of Australia. *United We Stand,* which began as a grass roots local event in Queensland, is now Australia's largest outreach event, uniting over 30,000 young people on one night at the same time, in different locations and seeing thousands saved. We haven't even touched on the *Academy,* which started just four years ago with five students here in Queensland and now has opened in six other locations, with more to come.

We are grateful for that cathedral, for the men and women who built it in years gone by. They are our heroes, the brave and bold ones who dared. We are also grateful for what God is building now. It's new and fresh and it's a different pattern, never seen before. So go ahead with great courage. Look back and say thank you and then grab your pencil and paper and get ready to create that new thing that's burning inside of you.

ESSENTIAL 11

Carry your corner of the mat

Although people might not admit it out loud, there is an unspoken understanding that success looks like putting your name in lights by building the biggest, fastest and most well-known ministry. Ask a lot of younger people today and they would love to be famous YouTubers or well-known entrepreneurs. However, we often think about the story in Mark 2:1-12 of the paralysed guy, who was carried to Jesus by four men. We often focus our attention on the paralysed man and how he was lowered down through the roof of the house and of Jesus' response to him, offering salvation first and healing second. But the real heroes of this story are the four friends who each carried a corner of the mat. We are not told any details about these men. They are nameless. They are faceless. But it was their persistent faith that brought about a miracle that day. With sweat rolling into their eyes, they had carried their paralysed friend for who knows how long, to get him to where Jesus was. They hoisted this heavy, full-grown man up the stairs onto the roof of the house. They took a risk, made a hole in the roof of a house whose owner they probably didn't know and with every last bit of energy, carefully lowered him to the ground right in front of Jesus. Jesus didn't look up and call out to thank the men, telling them what a good job they had done. The crowd's eyes were never on them, only on the paralysed man who suddenly appeared in front of them. Nobody applauded these nameless men.

Applause and accolades ruins more leaders today than almost anything else. The crowd could have been annoyed with them for interrupting their time with Jesus and the owner of the house might have been annoyed for the hole in his roof. We don't know if these men got to hang around to see the miracle, but even if they did, they happily took back row seats. They never made it about themselves.

Every time we read this passage, it speaks prophetically to us of the kind of leaders God is looking for right now. He is looking for those willing to give it all, pay the price, lay down their life and never ask for any recognition in return. This kind of call, the carrying of a paralysed, lost and broken generation to Jesus, with no thought to how we might benefit out of it, is what will truly change lives. One's true motive is very quickly identified by asking if we would be willing to serve Jesus and this generation, even if we never get one word of thanks or recognition.

There is a price to not being brash enough to push our way onto some stages and into certain green rooms. We marvel at some people's ability to talk themselves up and push their way in. They mix with the right people, hype up their posts, saying the right words until they get onto the stage they have been eyeing off. They make much of themselves making much about Jesus. Sadly, for the most part, people follow along like sheep, believing the hype. For a while, those that shout the loudest seem to get their way. But only for a while because we've seen the true fruit of this kind of behaviour – it might serve them to build a platform but it does nothing to serve this generation.

One of the deepest core values that we embrace is to never make this journey about us, or make a name for ourselves. We never agreed to lead *Youth Alive* with the goal in mind to become Christian celebrities.

Mother Teresa[11] never went to Calcutta as a brilliant strategy to get famous.

When we went to *Soul Survivor* conference in the UK to see Mike Pilavachi, two things stood out to us; there was no front row full of important guests and the green room was a makeshift tent with toasters to cook your own toast and caramel slice from a packet bought from the supermarket to nibble on. Our hearts leapt and we knew we were home! Mike kept the main game the main game – and that was seeing a generation encounter Jesus. It's not wrong to look after guests and Mike certainly did that well, but we should never crave that front row seat.

The four men who carried their friend to Jesus each played their part, not one of them trying to be more important than the other. If those four men were not in complete unity, if one decided to drop his end of the mat, the paralysed man would have fallen to the ground.

United We Stand has taught us more about true unity than anything else we have been a part of. To see the body of Christ all doing their part, shoulder-to-shoulder, has been one of the most awe-inspiring moments in our ministry. UWS forces us all to lay down our agenda and grab a corner of the mat. Youth pastors from every location and

---

[11] Mother Teresa, a Roman Catholic saint and Nobel laureate known for her missionary work with the poor in India

denomination join forces and it's a beautiful sight to see. What speaks volumes to us is the buses lined up in the carpark, each with a different youth group name on the side and to see youth leaders from the local churches serving side by side. That's God's people walking together, each carrying their corner of the mat, bringing our hurting and broken generation to Him. THAT is what miracles are made of.

Real deal unity is absolutely beautiful. It unlocks miracles and the power of God. The Bible is clear that where there is unity, God commands a blessing. That word command means to give orders, to tell, direct. God loves unity so much that when He sees it, He can't stay seated on His throne. He stands to His feet, peers down at that display of unity, His heart beating faster and His mouth smiling wide. He shouts at all the blessings flying around His throne and directs, tells, orders those blessings to go to that group of people RIGHT NOW. *Bless every one of them*, He shouts and they make their way down.

A few weeks ago a very prominent leader told us *Youth Alive* had the one thing everybody wanted. We were fascinated as to what this one thing was that we supposedly had. '*Unity*' he said.

We were floored. His words clashed, were all back to front, hypocritical even. We don't own unity. Unity isn't something one person has because if that were so it would not be unity anymore.

There was another big movement that we suggested join forces with us - *let's do something together. It would be healthy and powerful for all the young people. But who would own it they asked? Well! Nobody. Everybody. But someone has to wear the crown, they answered.* They walked away because they wanted to wear the crown. So we walked away, sad and shaking our heads because we don't want to wear the crown. Why does one body have to wear the crown?

True unity does something inside us that's almost more powerful than what it looks like on the outside. It reveals our true motives, because true unity means not one person wears the crown. It will test how much we really want it because it can only happen if our own agenda is laid aside. If the truth be told, personal agendas get in the way a lot these days.

Unity looks like kids getting on buses from every youth group and driving to one place to be together. It looks like one youth group flinging open its doors and welcoming in a whole heap of other youth groups. It looks like every denomination, coming together to pray. Unity sounds like a band that's made up of musicians from a bunch of different youth groups. It's a stage shared by this youth pastor and that youth pastor, who are actually really good friends.

But unity is no longer unity when one youth group or person tries to own it. It's ALL of us, dancing to the same beat, sharing the same stage and loving kids together and it's working just as hard when NOBODY sees.

It looks a lot like *United We Stand*.

It's 30,000 young people and youth pastors and leaders coming together on one night at the same time all around the country, uniting to lift up the only name that counts – Jesus. Who owns *United We Stand*? Nobody. Everybody. You do. Every young heart in this nation does. We might facilitate it, but it's not owned by Cameron and Renèe. You don't see our names on anything. There's no boss, no name in lights, except the one that counts – Jesus. It's all in together, moving in the same direction and nobody is wearing the crown except Him.

ESSENTIAL 12

Turn up consistently and for the long haul

When you do something for a long time, you get really good at it. Our young people are in desperate need of youth pastors and leaders who really know what they are doing because they've done it for a long time. They deserve that. They need that.

Some people ask us why we are still doing *Youth Alive*, now we are also lead pastors of a church. Nobody else has ever run *Youth Alive* in two states before. Nobody has run *Youth Alive* as long as we have before. When God is still on you for something, you can feel it in your bones. When God's anointing is on you for a task, there is a grace that makes you float along. We know what that feels like. We also know what it feels like when God's anointing has lifted. The task becomes a burden, a weight that makes you feel as though you are suffocating. It presses down on you and you can't wait to hand it over. Yet with every passing year, we still feel graced to do what we do. But the second we don't, we will be the first to cheerfully pass it on.

In a world where things are changing incredibly fast, predictability and longevity bring a sense of safety. People like that in our lives are so important. Like my Nanna and Pa. Every New Years we'd walk into their house to the smell of deep fried Ollen Bollen and dripolator coffee. Christmas was butter cake that melted in your mouth, a tin of chocolates passed around just one more time while the wooden candle-man sat puffing on his pipe from the window sill. There was a sense of security and well-being, a warmth about walking up to that door, seeing Nanna and Pa in the window before they knew we were there.

There were hugs and kisses on both cheeks and unconditional love every single time. They loved that we all turned up every year. With four children, 13 grandchildren and 20+ great grandchildren, that's a lot of turning up. We could always count on them turning up for other family events, every Birthday, Weddings, Births, Christmas. As predictable as the sun rising, Nanna and Pa were always present. When Pa died and a few years later, Nanna also, the world didn't seem quite right with them not in it anymore.

There's something powerful about turning up consistently and for the long haul in young people's lives. When you aren't about building your own platform but growing fruit in young people, you don't mind how long or how often you need to keep turning up. In a world that is ever-changing so quickly it makes you dizzy, so we are the ones this generation can hold on to when they need to steady themselves.

We once heard someone saying that kids need quality over quantity, when it comes to spending time. We couldn't disagree more. They need quantity just as much as quality. They need us to show up hard and often. It doesn't always have to be entertainment and fireworks.

Life happens in the in-between, the mundane, when we're not really looking. It happens in a conversation in the car or sitting at a music rehearsal. It happens when we take them for an ice-cream at Maccas or a stroll on the beach.

We've noticed that a lot of youth pastors move on quickly to become a campus pastor. There's nothing wrong with this, but when the pattern seems to be to rush people through youth ministry, it unwittingly devalues youth. It becomes a stepping stone that one must leap over quickly, a so-called necessary step to reach real deal ministry – whatever that real deal is. But we would argue that Kids Ministry is a real deal. Youth Ministry is a real deal. It's not one to get to the other, like eating your vegetables to get to dessert. Why can't one be called to youth ministry? Or kids ministry? A hero friend of ours is a rule-breaker. On the weekend he dons the black and white garb of an Anglican Minister, but mostly he ministers to youth pastors, leaders and young people themselves. At the age of almost 60, he is a sorely needed father to youth. They flock to him; tens and thousands of them. He travels the world talking to them. Who says he can't? Or shouldn't? Who says we can't? Or shouldn't? Who makes the rules about how this 'should' look?

We've watched youth ministries go through youth pastors every few years and we've seen the fruit of it. It destabilises the team, which destabilises the youth. Since youth are the engine room and future of any church, think about where that will lead. We need people like us to be fathers and mothers in the faith. We're not asking you to stay for 20 years like us, or a lifetime like our friend. But longer than one or two. Enough time to build something and burrow deep into the lives of those in your care.

Please don't feel you are done after only a few years. Please stay. Our young people need to look through the window and see the warmth and safety of familiar people who will open their doors over and over and say welcome home.

ESSENTIAL 13

Don't live life collecting recognition

Her name was Jaye and she was fierce and tender all at once behind her microphone and a guitar. She was only 17 when she came to us, accidentally falling into the role of music director in our youth group in Adelaide. Our previous guy had moved on suddenly and left a large space to fill, much larger than Jaye. She stood in his shadow, tiny and trembling on the outside but large and capable on the inside. It was a little flame that burned inside her at first but the fuel of encouragement soon turned it into something bigger. Week after week she showed up, with her over-sized guitar. She grew into the role, like a child filling up the spaces in their school shoes. She owned the stage like a girl boss, not because she thought she was good but she could sense this gift God had given her and because we kept telling her it was so. Like a seed that sprouts in the winter sun, her gift began to take shape and form and become something lovely.

Jaye began writing songs and with each one a beautiful memory was attached. Some were written at the altar at youth camp. Others came from the word Cameron preached. Each became an anthem, a prophetic utterance. What God was doing through Jaye became too big for our youth hall. The sound spilled out and made its way to the main church and eventually to churches and worship leaders in other states.

The whole while we would tell her the same thing. *We are so proud of you. We are your greatest cheer squad. When you're up there, nobody is cheering you on louder than we will be. Go far. Go hard.*

That is truly how we felt. For us, it is never about the recognition. It's not about our name or our face in lights. We've seen people clamber over others to make themselves greater, higher, recognised. This is not Jesus' way. Leadership is lending your shoulders for others to climb on. It's planting trees for shade that you may never sit under. We want our team members to go further and higher and wider than we've ever been. It makes us proud. Life is so much better when you live it to give recognition away.

We feel the same way about our Public staff. After Sundays, we feel like proud parents. When they preach, we lean forward on our seats a little and smile really hard. When they get messages and thank you's, we don't compare them to us or feel insecure or keep them down so we can feel up. No! Quite the opposite. Go team go! Nobody is cheering you on louder than us.

We have to fight against this innate human selfishness to be seen and recognised, to be the one holding the crown. We have a generation hooked on self gratification and pumped up on praise. It's up to us to model a different way, to get back to planting trees under whose shade we will never sit. As much as the world of social media has been a blessing, it has also fed our egos, made them plump with pride. Scrolling feeds has become an exhausting bragfest of competitive self branding.

We have always found success in a different place than ourselves. The success of those we disciple is the greatest reward. We rise by lifting others and the real heroes are those who are intent on making this a better place for all people. Great leadership is about making others better as a result of your presence.

ESSENTIAL 14

There is power in sitting with someone in the dark

Sometimes we watch things happen to others that break us apart in so many places, in so many different ways, that they can't be fixed all at once. But rather than rushing to the rescue and grabbing the dustpan and broom to sweep up and discard the evidence of a broken heart, the most powerful thing we can do is sit with them, in the dark.

There is so much power in sitting with someone in the dark. It's one thing to be there when celebrating but it's quite another to be the one to watch a heart crack in a million pieces. But people never forget the ones who were brave enough to stay. The ones who heard the stifled sobs, the angry questions, who have no answers except an offer of comfort. The truth is our youth are not looking for answers, but to know that someone loves them enough to be there for them.

One of our youth boys was losing one of his parents. In the most tragic of circumstances, his parent was breathing their last. While the sun outside was shining and kids were carrying backpacks and shouting at one another as they left school, this boy's life was turning dark and sad and quiet. But while I sat here writing, Cameron was there.

There are two times in life when it is imperative for us to be with our young people and our team. It's during the highest of highs and in the lowest of lows, but especially the lows. I'm not talking about one hour or one day or one week. This boy will need us for the next year, maybe years.

That night, when it was all happening, Cameron called him and his words covered the boy, like a warm blanket, a little bit of comfort on the coldest of nights.. If you're not sure if it's your place or not, do it anyway. We are better off over- caring than not caring enough. *I'm here for you*, he said. *Call me the second you need me.* Then he prayed. Broken, desperate words. There was not much at the other end of the line but this boy will never, ever forget that somebody cared for him in his darkest moment.

We've done this many times, dealt with the darkest and most private of moments in people's lives. We have been in the room when a son's life support was turned off. We watched as the boy's mother climbed up on his body and laid over him as he took his last breath, hoping against hope that by some miracle her life, her beating heart, could bring him back to her.

We've sat in lounge rooms when young people unlock their souls and whisper confessions of abuse. We've walked besides young girls for months, years, tortured, taunted and controlled by an eating disorder that gnawed away at their mind as well as their body. We were honoured to be asked to sit on the front row at the funeral of one of our leader's mums. We've watched young people wrestle with their sexuality and no matter what path they chose, have remained beside them, offering love and friendship without condition.

As we sit beside others, sharing their darkest moments, there is something we know that they have most likely forgotten. That even the dark must eventually give in to the light. The sun will rise and the long dark night will be but a distant memory. They won't want to hear that at the time, they won't be able to imagine anything else but the pitch black of their soul. This is why we must sit with them. The dark is really scary on your own. But if you have a friend to share it with, someone you can feel beside you even if you can't see their face, then some of the fear will subside and they'll feel that this black will perhaps not swallow them after all. We should stay no matter how long it takes. It could be an hour or a day, but some dark nights go on much longer. We mustn't give up and walk away when it does. I ask you, even though these young people might not have the words to tell you, please don't walk away. This is true leadership. This is real care, sitting with someone in the dark, until the dawn breaks and hope floods in again.

So back to our darling boy, who was facing a wall of grief. Cameron is in the room praying. He stands back and hopes that some of the grief will land on his big shoulders since it's much too heavy for a young boy to carry alone. Over the next weeks and months, we will be there for him. His squad leaders will call him and pick him up for youth. They'll call just to say hi and take him out for ice-cream and Top Golf and car rides. If we could, we would take away the burdens some of our youth have to carry. We would carry them ourselves if that was at all possible. Being there, for the long haul, is the most important thing in the world. You will be a little bit of light and colour and hope for them. Jesus says He is close to the broken-hearted and I believe that hope comes in the form of those charged with their care.

What you will need the most during these times is emotional resilience. It is our privilege for God to use us in this way, to help carry others, to offer to hold on to a corner of their burden and walk together for a while. Caring can hurt sometimes but it is a bittersweet part of humanity, to be able to share it and partake of it together. It requires us to think of someone else over ourselves, to be strong and resilient. To be the soft place where they can land, a safe space where they can cry. We've just watched this boy say goodbye to his father. It was gut wrenching and painful. But Cameron stood, tender but strong, a pillar of strength and beacon of hope in the dark. When we walked away, it was time to debrief because that's a part of emotional resilience too. There's something about the hearts of pastors and leaders, which makes them incredibly strong and apt to tear all at once.

So each day we check in on one another. *Are you doing okay? Let's chat.* For as much as we need to be there for others, we need people to be there for each other as well. To be emotionally resilient, we need to be able to sit with discomfort, let go of having the answers and engage in self-care. We need to know where our boundaries lie, where the line is between let me help and the times you need to step away. Surround yourself with good company. But most of all, remember we are not their saviour, only Jesus can do that.

ESSENTIAL 15

The story we tell is the culture we create

S tories have creative power and social media is an incredible gift, an open book, a blank page, where we get to tell our story. The words we use from the platform tell our story and the words we speak off stage do too. The story we tell creates the culture we live in.

Many youth pastors are doing an incredible job and seeing great results but the story is told to boast. Like a waft coming from a closed bin, you can smell it. They use their ministry to generate fame; pictures of themselves preaching to fish for more opportunities; feigning authenticity to heighten their self-importance; exaggerating numbers to project an image of success. If this is the story you tell, this is a culture you create, where fame means you've made it, the stage is coveted, vulnerability is hidden and numbers create worth. If this is the bed you make, you won't find it very comfortable to lie in. Before long you will find your team fighting for fame too, vying for the stage, real issues left undealt with and a push and hustle for bigger and better.

Our story is not told for everybody else. We do it for our youth and church family and if anyone else is interested, then they are most welcome to listen. You won't hear us speak of crowds and hype and numbers because these are not the things we value. We value people and what happens when their story becomes part of our wider story. We value the small things and the things of character. We know that to build a strong youth we must build strong young people. We value honesty and even brokenness. It's not about us but all about them and God is in the middle of it all.

For us it's team who are family, shoulder to shoulder, pulling together in the same direction. It's not one above the other but all in together. We celebrate the one who sweeps as much as the one who preaches. They are listening, our young, wide-eyed ones. Just as legendary fables are told to pass on lessons and values, so the stories we tell with our words and with our posts pass silent lessons to our youth. The lessons gathered over weeks, months and years weave and build and blur together until they become our culture.

Ours is one we are proud to live inside.

PART 2
TRANSFORMING LEADERS

ESSENTIAL 16

Transformational leaders win hearts

Here is the first key to understanding this wild, complex but beautiful Gen Z. They don't respond to an authoritarian style of leadership. However, they don't mind you being firm with them, but that is entirely different to authoritarianism. They admire strong leaders who aren't pushovers, but ones that at the same time show incredible humility and authenticity. With Gen Z, respect comes not because of your title or position but because you have truly earned it by who you are.

They will be utterly loyal and look up to leaders who are more concerned with their development than what they can do. These are transformational leaders - that is, those concerned first and foremost with the true heart-change of people. They will be demotivated by a focus on achievement and tasks, especially if those things benefit you. They can sniff out leaders who are in it for self-promotion and success, even if done subtly. They are not wowed by the ambitious pushing of our own agenda, but are looking for somebody they consider worth following.

Relationships are of the highest importance with Gen Z's but they also want to make a difference and serve something bigger than themselves. They are moved by strong and fresh vision and want to be challenged and changed as they follow you. They may not want to be besties with you, but they do want to know that you care about who they are and the things they care about.

The impact and influence you have on them will not come about because of your title or position. They won't be impressed by another social media posting of you preaching. It's the non sexy things, like spending time with them, that will build the most incredible amount of respect and therefore influence in their lives.

Gen Z wants to be transformed themselves as they follow you. It's about engaging their hearts, which will lead them to commit to the vision and in the process, empower them to fulfill their God-given potential.

This is exactly what Russell and Sam did with our leadership team. We were all inextricably bound together, working toward a vision that was not about one man or one woman, but was about changing a generation together for God. As we did that, we were transformed in the process and we each found our God calling. It was a sweet, prophetic and divine balance that we still strive to model in our leadership today.

It's about working together, towards a greater good. That's why every youth ministry should serve and attend something bigger than itself. It maintains a healthy focus, opens up our God-view of the world and gives our young people a taste of Him. It shows them that God and His Kingdom is far bigger than the four walls of one church or youth ministry. Never be afraid to open up your leaders and youth group to other people and ministries. Some leaders keep them away for fear they will lose them. But this generation respects leaders who want the best for them and who want to develop them.

They won't care whether 100 or 200 kids rock up to youth on a Friday night. In fact they will wonder at your obsession with numbers. Leave those as healthy goals that you can discuss and pray about with your leadership team, but let those numbers be motivators and not drivers.

A lot of pastors find a teenage audience scary and intimidating but we find them the most deeply amazing humans we will ever get the privilege of leading. The secret is to win their hearts. Once you have done that, they are beautiful, soft and mouldable and they'll want to take on the world by your side.

ESSENTIAL 17

Real discipleship is transformational

If we had to pick our top essential, this would be it. This is the Holy Grail, the beginning and end of a great youth ministry. If you do nothing else you will still see incredible fruit.

Have regular discipleship with your leaders.

This principle was a key element to building our youth ministry and we literally built our home around it. Our first block of land was tiny, but it was ours and we had saved hard for it. It was snuggled in a gully, with gum trees as a backdrop. We built a humble cottage and sacrificed a backyard so we could build a bigger lounge, to fit our leader's discipleship meetings there. We didn't think twice about making plans like this for our youth team. They were not a tack on or an after-thought, sewn onto the side of our life like a button on a jacket. These young people were not a job, a 9-5 affair. They were our life, our people, our team. They were front and centre of our days and plans. They were everything to us because we were building something together, for God. They were not a group to be managed, but partners in our God

Call. So of course we would build our home to accommodate them, every last one of them.

So our tiny cottage had an oversized lounge. It didn't make sense to a lot of people who visited our home but it made perfect sense to us. That lounge, so simple, so plain, was where dreams were birthed and prayers had creative power. It was where we laughed, ate and planned camps. We knew we'd never have enough chairs so we paid extra for 'golden underlay' when laying the carpet, so it was extra soft to sit on. We almost can't believe it, looking back. 'Golden underlay'! We hope you feel the same about your team. That you would be prepared to pay extra for 'golden underlay' because their precious comfort means that much to you too.

So every fortnight, we annoyed our neighbours, filling up the street with cars, all sorts of pretty average cars, most of them with P plates. Our leadership team would pile in, Maccas, cokes and crunchie bars in hand and Bibles stuffed under their arms. They were special nights. They were an unruly group who perhaps were not all willing to be friends at first but we had two things in common. We all loved Jesus and we all wanted to change a generation. That became the thread that held us together. Nobody could fall away, even if they tried. They eagerly showed up at our home. We ran those nights full of love for one another and worship to God.

Discipleship was always compulsory. If you were a leader, you had to come, and nobody minded. They wanted to be there. There were rules to follow. You need a few rules and this was one of ours. If for some reason, something unforeseeable happened to prevent their attendance, they had to text and let us know. Otherwise it was all in.

We'd begin with a little 'housekeeping', sharing briefly about what was coming up at Youth followed by pastoral care. We'd print off every leader's small group list and check in on which young people had been missing from youth. Everyone knew we could ask about any young person at any time. We held them highly accountable for every young person in their charge. We taught them to value every name on their list because every name is a young person in our care.

Housekeeping only ever took a maximum of 15 minutes. The remainder of the night was dedicated to what we were really there to do, to love and guide, encourage and feed. This was the 'discipling' part of 'discipleship'. It was raw, real and followed the ebbs and flows of what God was saying to us at the time. We didn't follow a program or a book, though we are not saying this doesn't have its place at times. We've found that culture is more caught than taught. A six week growth track or leadership course can sometimes feel forced. We don't sit our kids down for six weeks and teach them about life in the Bennett household. It's learnt and caught by being with one another over time. It seeps out in the things we say, the things we don't say, those we do and those we won't allow. Culture and values are moved like osmosis, from our heart to theirs, with slow exposure over time, during the normal rhythms of doing life together.

Discipleship is an important part of that. We'd share whatever we felt God was saying. It was always fresh and relevant and we made it personal to them. We didn't share about leading better or growing our youth group. It was about matters of the heart and what was going on deep inside of them. At the end of the night, we would turn the lights down and sing or pray or just be quiet. Sometimes we would lay hands on them and prophecy. There were usually tears, the kind that comes from ugly crying and it wasn't because of us or what we said. It was because God was always reaching down into the depths of their being, healing, comforting, restoring. In that oversized lounge room, they were no longer leaders. They were young people, letting God in, inviting Him into the deepest recesses of who they were.

What happened in those years, in that lounge, was sacred. It was so honest and powerful that it spilled over into the entire youth ministry. Leaders went back to their life groups and imitated what they had learned and practiced on those nights. Friday night, when the altar was crammed with youth lined up waiting for a touch from God, our leaders prayed over them the way we prayed over them at discipleship.

We didn't tell them how to be leaders. We showed them. It wasn't do as we say, it was do as we do. Over the years, the times we shared became precious memories. Nobody wanted to leave our youth team, and others wanted to join. God did something really special in those years. We celebrated birthdays together. We stood beside them at altars as they said 'I do' at their weddings and were the first to visit at the hospital after they gave birth to their babies. We were honoured to be asked to sit beside them at funerals of those they dearly loved. We cried when they cried. We celebrated when they celebrated. We went through the valleys and mountains of life side by side. The youth ministry grew and young lives were forever changed, not because of us, but because of them. Those young leaders who sat on the 'golden underlay' carpet, in our over-sized lounge room.

ESSENTIAL 18

Have conversations that change people's lives

hen we were building the youth ministry in Adelaide, we spent most of our time with the leaders. Now our leadership teams are filled with young people who are muddling their way through their own journey, trying to help other youth just a few years younger than themselves. They are a work in progress and we need to be patient with them.

We have loved and discipled them as though they were our very own, orphans adopted into our hearts. In reality they all had parents, but at the tender age of 18,19 and early 20's, they still offered themselves up for guidance and love and nurture. Graduating high school doesn't suddenly make them experts and they certainly haven't graduated from navigating through many of their own issues.

To this day, the parents of our leaders still thank us. Just a few years ago, we were at one of their weddings. We had cared for this leader and his sister for years, holding them steady through the turbulent waters of their parents' rocky relationship breakdown and divorce. On this day the father came and found us in the car park. He threw his arms around us and held on for what might be considered way too long. But we understood the silent words that were being transferred to us in a sort of osmosis. *Thank you.* But he couldn't utter those words because he knew they didn't seem adequate for what he wanted to say.

Those leaders we discipled all those years ago are still in connection with us today. The principles on which we built our team are still the same ones we use when we disciple pastors and leaders around the country.

Discipling the hearts of others ends up changing them and us but only if done correctly and carefully, because these hearts of ours are made of stuff which make them incredibly strong and sensitive, making us sometimes wish there was a road map to navigate them.

We want you to know that the conversations you have, with the special people you call 'team', are invaluable. Also life-changing and sometimes difficult. It's the important conversations, the ones that dive deep into what's unseen from the top. It is also essential to remember that these young hearts are still learning, still working it all out. At times they will find themselves out in the deep, out of control and struggling to stay afloat. This is when they need us. Our conversations become a lifeline, a safe place for them to grab onto while steadying themselves until they find their feet again.

A few years into being youth pastors at *Solid Rock* in Adelaide, it came to our attention that one of our leaders who was on the music team, had been going out partying and getting drunk. One of our staff members wanted us to come down hard. They felt this was not acceptable and it did not reflect how we wanted our youth leaders to behave. It was not a good example to the young people. This was true. However we have found that coming down hard, writing people off, banning them from serving, is too harsh an approach that does not usually reap good rewards.

We have high standards for those who serve on a team, but we also have an equal if not greater measure of love for them. We have learnt to look below the surface at the why and then love them back to God and the person He created them to be. For has not grace been extended to us in liberal measure and therefore can we not also extend the same grace? So this staff member wanted us to take him off team and send him to attend the young adult ministry.

We had another plan.

We caught up with this young man and had one of those conversations. The life-line kind. We told him we knew what he had been up to, and that we loved him. We knew he was hurting because growing up he had lost his dad and was acting out his hurt by partying and alcohol. We told him it's ok, that we were there for him and wanted him to get his heart fixed up. So we asked him to step off the team for three months, not as punishment but as an offering of time to heal. We wanted him to come to discipleship and youth and catch up with us every fortnight during those three months.

The staff member sighed and crossed his arms at our leniency. But we held firm and it did something amazing. It made that young man rise to want to be the best version of himself. When he thought he would be written off, we offered grace and he couldn't resist. During those three months words were exchanged between us that were like liquid gold, putting back the broken pieces of his heart. He became unstuck and unbroken. After three months, he returned to team, not perfect but perfectly loved, seen fully and still fully accepted and acceptable.

That young man stayed a leader in the youth ministry for the next four years before becoming a leader in young adults. When the time came for him to get married, we were honoured to stand before he and his now wife and perform the ceremony. More than 15 years later we are all still friends. He is a wonderful husband and father. We are so proud that all it took were conversations. Simple, easy, but loving words. So the right words spoken at the right time and with the right heart lead to miracles.

ESSENTIAL 19

Small groups are a training ground for leadership development

We have led so many small groups these past 20 years, we have lost count. We've been involved because we believe in them and the power and place they hold in people's lives. They are a staple, like meat and three veg for a meal, nourishing and feeding the soul in an important way, more than a large gathering can. We believe in large gatherings too, but there is something about smaller ones that fills a needed space in people's lives - the space that's only filled by connection and love and being truly seen. One can't always be seen in a large group. But a more intimate setting provides a space for everyone's voice to be heard and valued.

There are many reasons why we believe in small groups, for leaders as well as young people and we must fight to keep the small group ministry alive and thriving in a time and place where busyness is squeezing the most valuable traditions out.

One reason we must not give up the practice of small groups is because of the way it develops leaders like no other practice in the church. It grows leaders in a thousand different ways. It teaches them to consistently care for others. It gives them a little platform to practice putting together messages and devotions and mini sermons and then delivering it to willing ears. It's a space for leaders to be responsible for a program and to outwork the larger church vision within that space.

It gives an opportunity for a leader to lead worship, a safe place to develop this skill. Even if they are not going to be the church's next rising musical star, it's another arrow to pop into their quiver of skills.

It's the most natural and healthy way for new leaders to be identified and developed. It also teaches the leader how to reproduce themselves in these new, young, fresh ones coming through. We always tried to team up a leader with an assistant. The aim was for the leader to assist them to be ready to take on their own group. If the current small group grows large enough, we could then split the group in half and the assistant would become the main leader. Each leader would then choose a new assistant, so our leadership teams multiplied. If someone wasn't ready for an assistant role, we would make them a key worker until they were ready to become an assistant.

Small groups teach leaders to be faithful with the little, because if they can be faithful with the little, then we could place a bit more into their hands and trust them with more responsibility. Being a connect group leader forces them to get out of their comfort zone, make phone calls and visits and develop a trusting relationship with parents. It's a place where you can observe how they look after the house that hosts have generously opened up to them.

Does the leader lead the young people and teach them how to treat the resource that's been loaned to them? This alone will tell you a lot. Do they ask the young people to take their shoes off at the door and say hello to the house hosts? Do they treat the furniture with respect and eat in one place, over a plate? Do they leave the place better than when they arrived? Do they say 'thank you for having me' on the way out the door? All these things are important.

Is being a small group leader a job they can tick off each week or do they carry the heart of it? Do they understand the young lives they can change if they are only willing to dig deep into them? Do the leaders allow their lives to be intertwined with their group members? Do they gather them, like chickens to a hen, stretching out their wings of protection during the week as well? Have they created a sense of family that draws these young people together and gives them a soft space to land? Do they love them and allow them to be themselves?

We know that's a lot of questions but we encourage you to take the time to reflect. There is no better training ground to develop leaders then the small group space. And better leaders means more lives transformed.

ESSENTIAL 20

Raising the next generation of leaders is a priority

As the youth ministry in Adelaide began to grow, we realised there was a desperate need for more leaders. It was like a train, running at full speed with a momentum all its own. Whispers of what was happening in the youth hall was reaching the young adults so one by one, they started coming to us, asking to join the leadership team. That is until the young adult pastor got wind of it. He didn't want to see his people being siphoned off one by one, into the vortex of *Solid Rock*. So he put a stop to it, closed the door, battened down the hatches so to speak. *Solid Rock* was madly growing and we desperately needed more leaders to meet the ever-growing needs of our young people.

A valuable lesson that has become our mantra, is when the resource is tight, rather than complaining or blaming, it forces you to be creative and innovative. These are desirable giftings to have, because it means you will never be stopped by not having enough. The closing of the doors was the best option at that time. We looked around for a solution and realised it was sitting right within our very midst and the answer was our current year 12's.

We have never been a big fan of student leaders. You might totally disagree, which is fine, because it doesn't mean you can't develop your students in other areas, like giving them a go at a 'young guns' preaching night. Or training them up in the youth band or having them co-lead a song or two. They can show leadership by helping look after the younger ones and assisting with planning for youth camps. But full-blown leadership we steer clear of for a number of reasons. Sometimes a little power goes to their head and they like to wield it like a lightsaber a little too freely above the heads of others. They're still babies themselves and need leading, loving and nurturing. They have their own responsibilities, like working hard and achieving the best they can at school. Student leaders create a hierarchy amongst their peers like only teenagers seem to know how to do. Insecurities come out like cat claws and questions asked such as, *why did you get chosen?* Besides, we don't really want our 13 year old being lead by a 15 year old, no matter how good they are.

However, as Year 12 came to an end, we decided to invest in a bunch of them, pull them under our wing and get them ready for leadership the year after. There was a sense of family by this stage, like we were really getting somewhere and making a difference in young people's lives. It seemed that nearly every Year 12 wanted to stay the following year so we invited them to join a fortnightly leadership development gathering at our house called *Boost*. We have no idea why we called it that, but let's be clear 'Boost Juice' was not heard of at the time.

Boost operated for six weeks and was in the same vein as our leaders' discipleship gatherings at our house. It wasn't a course or a list or a bunch of leadership do's and don'ts, but was typical of how we work. Culture and who we are, can't be taught from a book. We're not big believers in courses and discipleship DNA's. Leadership is about heart and culture and we find these things are more caught than taught. It's about the things we say over and over. It's about the things we do and the things we don't do. It's a bit like raising kids. We don't sit them down each night and preach 'how to be kids 101'. We don't put a manual in their hands while we read ours and stick to lists and rules and points and sermons. We do life together. We talk. We learn along the way. We love how Deuteronomy talks about chatting about the Bible on our way, while we are doing the ordinary stuff called life.

Boost kind of looked like that but on steroids because we couldn't have 20 almost young adults live in our house! So they came every second Wednesday night and we talked about being called and serving and how this looked a whole lot like family. We laid the expectations on the table and boundaries as well because these are healthy and necessary. We shared devotions with them and prayed over them. We prophesied, they cried and sometimes we cried too. We could feel it; the weight. The beautiful weight of a young life called by God and we were privileged to watch them offer their lives in surrender.

We got down in the mess with them, like you do when you play in the sand with your kids. We built castles of dreams and were sometimes able to push back the dirt to see what was really happening underneath. We listened, we talked and they shared. They felt safe with us. Like it didn't matter who they were or what they said, we'd always love them.

We did love them, believed in them and who they were and who they wanted to be. They began to feel like they could fly. We fed them pancakes and pizza because there's something special about being around the table together. We knew we weren't just spending time with them, we were doing something far more valuable. We were investing. There's a difference, you know, and therein lies the secret.

Some leaders just spend time with new leaders, like that is the right thing to do. They hand them a leaders manual, inform them of the task at hand. But spending time gives you equal return for what you put in. However, investing is a whole other thing. We saw our time, our love, our belief and opening our house door as an investment. Because for the little bit we put in, we got so much back. Through investing into their lives a little, they went on to impact and change the lives of many more young people. It was returned to us, repaid over and over again in so many ways. How can you measure getting into the trenches with 10 or 20 or 30 young people and then watching them get into the trenches with another 10 or 20 or 30. The multiplication effect is breathtaking.

We had already travelled a few years with most of them, but at the end of the six weeks, we had a conversation with each of them individually. We asked where their hearts were leading them and what they thought God wanted them to do. Some decided they weren't quite ready for leadership yet and we sent them off with massive hugs and love into the big wide world of young adulthood. But most of them wanted to stay. They were in. So once year 12 was completed, we paired each of them with an experienced leader. We didn't just pull names out of hats. We were thoughtful and intentional about who would work best with who. We fed them into our small group set up because systems aren't here to drive us, but serve us and small groups served us well, helping us raise leaders.

A few were ready to be assistant leaders immediately, but for the most part they began as key workers. They were like apprentices, learning the tools of the trade, taken under the wing of someone a bit further down the track than they were. They joined our discipleship training too; invited in like a new family member.

So it continued, the process of passing the baton, raising the next generation of leaders. The following year we repeated the process, and again the year after and the year after that.

ESSENTIAL 21

Take the clock off the wall

I love the way Cameron teaches the young leaders around him. He doesn't always use words. He shows. It's not always in meetings. He finds moments, just a few seconds here and there.

Wild and free spirited Si had been with us for almost two years. He raged against being stuffed into a box or hemmed in by rules and routine. He was learning about the Call of God, pressing heavy on him at times. But the God Call is an adventure and freedom when ordinary living just doesn't cut it. But sometimes he finds himself suffocating under the weight and he wants to escape. There's a fight going on the inside. My will or His (God's) will. He knows he's been put on this earth for a God purpose but it's human nature to count the cost.

Cameron understands Si because he is like him. He is the most non-pastorish pastor you could possibly find. He asks questions and challenges the status quo. He goes left when everyone else is going right. He pushes boundaries and loves finding others who are built the same way, taking them under his wing, pulling them alongside to show them who they are and all they are called to be.

Every Sunday we do set up and pack down for church. There is a love/hate relationship with the whole deal because there's always more and more boxes and piles of stacking to do. But while boxes are being stacked in towers to the ceiling, friendships are made as well. While we strip the school hall walls of art work and close curtains and mop floors, we laugh and learn about each other's history. Each Sunday, just before the service is about to start, Cameron can be seen whispering in Si's ear as he passes. It's always the same question. *Did we miss anything?* Si would shake his head. *Nope, we didn't. Look again,* Cameron would whisper.

The clock. Yes, the clock. Si would go and whisk the ugly school clock off the wall. But it's not really about the clock. It's Cameron teaching Si to see what he sees. Do as he does. Lead as he leads. It's the copying of the pattern, like Paul did for Timothy and Elijah for Elisha. It's taking the mantle from his shoulders and laying them on Si's. This is how leaders are made. Slowly, over time, as we show them the way.

Si's wife, Shani, told me the other day over coffee - *I think Cameron is teaching Si,* she said. Taking clocks off walls, picking up the mop, straightening chairs, picking up kids in your car, praying hard in the prayer meeting, are really heart lessons and preparation for what is ahead. It's because we see a man who is going to do great and mighty exploits for God. He will influence and lead and change a generation. But to do that tomorrow, he has to see that the clock needs taking off the wall today.

ESSENTIAL 22

When people don't have the same values as you, let them go

On the journey, some people you lead will shatter your heart into glass shards, because they think that the insides of a leader are made of far tougher stuff than it really is. Truth is, to be lovers of people means our hearts will be broken in a thousand ways. What makes us great leaders is the ability to pick up those pieces and not allow someone else to be sliced open on the sharp edges. It means swallowing poison and not allowing anyone else to taste the bitterness that we must endure. Sometimes it means swallowing a pill so large, it gets stuck in our throats and we want to choke, but we smile and take our pain behind closed doors. Pain is far more than just something that might happen. It's inevitable! It will take residence and space inside of you like black smoke, filling your lungs and taking your breath away. But our ability to which we can endure pain will determine how far and deep and wide our leadership will go.

This is what we've found. When others hand you a bitter ugly pill, it's because they don't understand their own pain. They don't know what to do with it, so it's easier for them to give it to you.

There are some leaders who, when we try to have an honest conversation with them, will get angry at us for pointing out their pain. You show them something they have spent their whole life stuffing down, the volcanic lava that's been bubbling underneath. You implore them to stop and listen and feel it. Or perhaps you did something wrong, made a mistake. Everyone makes mistakes. That's called being human. We have the right to talk about it, say sorry and be forgiven. But sometimes people don't want to accept your apology because it's easier to blame you than take responsibility themselves.

Actually there's not much that can't be fixed by conversation. Words can break and wound but words can also heal and mend. In a previous chapter we talked about miracles that words can take us too. But what do you do when the other person doesn't want to hear? They don't want to talk. They don't want to acknowledge the burning ash slowly consuming them from the inside. They are petrified of looking inward and letting go or both.

We had one such experience not long ago. We took a punt on someone, a risk. That's what leaders do. We don't mind getting our hands messy in the detail of someone's life. We have done it for 20 years. Where there is a trail of brokenness we revel in being allowed to reach into the muddy places, offer it up to God and watch Him form something incredible out of the mess. We thrive on deep conversations, the kind that go far beyond 'how are you?' and reach into the foundations of who they really are.

We knew this person had so much God potential, but they had spent a long time running and blaming, half-building things and giving up. *Walk with us, we said. We've been on this journey a long time. Let's build something great together.* This person said yes and willingly came, until it got too hard, until we began those conversations. So they built walls that our words bounced off, echoing back to us.

We tried everything. Our hearts were sad, because one cannot penetrate a wall that is so thick, it's hemmed them in for years. We shouted over the wall. *You can be free. Please. Let us help you.* But they said they knew better and they were quite fine thank you very much and they stayed behind the wall, in the fortress they had built. *You are wrong,* they said. But we knew it was not about us being wrong or them being right, or them being wrong or us being right. They had made it about that and cast blame, kicking and screaming like a child who refuses their vegetables, the very thing that will make them grow big and strong.

They made some mistakes, said they were sorry and we said it's ok, let's learn and move on. They dropped a few bricks from the wall and it gave us hope. But they made the same mistake again. This time it hurt other people. We jumped and we climbed, but we slid down the wall of the fortress they'd built. We felt like a defeated pile of nothing laying on the ground, but we got up, brushed ourselves off and realised this time we needed to walk away.

In those times where we have had to walk away, we've learned a lesson or two. We've learned that sometimes people don't share the same values as us. We deeply value honesty and hard work and honesty (yes we said it twice, because we really value it). We value ploughing the ground together, doing our part and helping others, even when it's hard.

We value taking responsibility and saying sorry and picking ourselves up and trying again. We value teachable hearts, humble hearts. But sometimes people value other things and that's ok. But when God has given you the permit and mandate to build, it's important to do it with people who share the same values. Otherwise it will feel more like a task, pushing a heavy trolley up an incline, instead of an enjoyable road trip with your best friends.

When you decide your values are different, you must be honest. Just because a conversation is difficult or they don't want to hear it, it's important to speak truth in love because being silent is worse. Have that conversation even when it's one-sided, and let them go. After you've said goodbye and parted ways, no matter how they behave or what they say on the way out the door, stay quiet. Hopefully you will experience nothing but kind partings, but life is not always roses and chocolate cake. Often people who have built these fortresses with their own behaviour, want to somehow pretend that you were the one who hemmed them in.

When we finally decided to let this person go, they were very unkind. They lashed out, their tongue and their actions whipping and cutting and slashing. They kept pushing the pill of their pain down our throat with blaming and unkind words. They unfriended us on social media, which to us is not a great deal different than a child stamping their foot on the ground and hoping it punishes you. But we should never return unkindness. Always be a bigger person.

Reputations have a way of catching up with people and we have learned that when your reputation is consistently good, people will not believe the lies of others. Being the bigger person means moving toward them every single time. That's not always easy, but then leadership is not about easy. It's swallowing that pill and smiling, even when it hurts and even when you don't deserve it.

Then there's truth. One of the best bits of advice we have heard of late is, *when other people ask why so-and-so has gone, don't lie*. Don't smooth over the quilt cover when everyone knows there's a crumpled up sheet underneath. Tell the most loving version of the truth. It's messy. Our values weren't the same. We had to let them go. Then gulp hard, smile and look around you at the crowd of faces still with you, for they are your people.

ESSENTIAL 23

Divine friendships outwork divine purposes

We believe in God bringing people together, supernaturally, to outwork His divine purposes. The Bible is full of God-breathed partnerships that resulted in the miraculous. From Elijah and Elisha, Mary and Elizabeth, Paul and Timothy to Abraham and Sarah, Moses and Aaron, and David and Jonathan.

From our twenty plus years in ministry, the majority of that in youth, we've seen how God builds relationally. We have never been lone-ranger type leaders. We have no interest in being the heroes in the story. We want people that we can build with. Looking back over our lives, to this day our very best of friends are those very same people we fought with in the trenches of ministry. We didn't just work together, we lived life together, in all of its glorious ups and downs, messes and delights.

While we lived out our Mondays to Sundays side by side, weeks collecting into months and years, what seemed mundane at the time began to look more like a miracle after all. We clocked in and out of our days. Prayer meetings, staff retreats, conferences, Sundays, staff meetings, youth. What seemed like the ordinary actually wasn't what it was at all because the extraordinary was buried within these ordinary days. Even now, after two decades, people from all over the country and beyond, recognise the deeply fierce connections of those of us who worked together in Adelaide. People tell us how they envy our friendships, which seem to go beyond anything they have ever seen or experienced.

One of the keys to the lifelong friendships that were built back then was that we weren't just building together – it was the *right* people building together. The leadership over us had a prophetic way of putting the right people in the right positions. It was the blend of people, the 'who was partnered with who'. Leadership decisions were not reactionary, or filling holes and spaces in church life with whoever seemed the nearest or closest fit. It's a gift, the ability to put the right people together in the right place, making something good into something great. It turns the ordinary into the extraordinary, the average into something breathtaking and incredible.

When we were first asked to take over the youth ministry at our church in Adelaide, we thought we were being demoted. The youth was not that strong at the time, so to be asked to oversee it seemed more like a silent vote that we were incapable of being given anything that was seen as valuable. Then we realised that the senior pastor's kids were teenagers and not attending youth. Suddenly the lights went on and it hit us in the face that the opposite was true. Although we had only ever run connect groups and Cameron was running *New Christians* and *New People* at the time, Russell suggested us because he didn't look at people with his natural eyes. All hopes were pinned on us, that we could turn the ship around and get the senior pastors' kids engaged in youth again. By then, we knew the importance of team. Not a blend of just anyone. The right and perfect God mix.

Almost a decade after moving to Queensland we knew it was time to plant a church. We started with 11 people in our lounge. If I am to be very honest, my courage failed me many times in those early days. Doubts of *who would want to join us* and *what if we don't succeed?* We were always on the look out for the divine connections we knew God would bring along. Looking back, we can see the pivotal moments when God sent people through our doors and straight into our hearts. They are names to you - Chloe and Danny, Bennie and Vanessa, Josh and Eden, Jake and Sarah, but to us they are gifts straight from Heaven. I always say God loves our staff meetings best, because we are the most unconventional lot who spend most of our time laughing, with Cameron the main culprit, of course. We work so incredibly hard but we enjoy each other's company so much, it never feels like work.

Rarely will it make sense, but you will feel it deep down. You'll get the *'I feel like they are meant to be with us'* vibes. They'll be strangers who feel like it was meant to be. They'll come when there's no money, no prestige, no lights or accolades. Hold these ones tight. They are ready to build for all the right reasons. Love them well. They are God's provision, His smile upon your adventure.

Here's the thing with divine partnerships – don't always look for the 'ready made'. Don't discount the diamonds in the rough, the ones who are hidden. Isn't that just like God? Didn't he pick David, hidden in the fields amongst the sheep? He chose Mary, the virgin girl with no experience of being a mother? He chose Moses, who stuttered and Peter, who had a big mouth? Heart means everything to God, so it does with us also. Don't be in a hurry to choose people to build with. Sit back, observe, give it time and room to breathe. Watch who God is on. Listen to the beat of your heart and the beat of theirs. Do they match? Are they in sync? Our prayer is that God liberally sprinkles our country with divine partnerships, because our young people do not have the time for us to be the only hero in their story.

ESSENTIAL 24

Don't be afraid of team conflict

There will be conflict on your team. It will be aimed at you and sometimes created by you. Sometimes it will be between your team and other times have nothing to do with you. It will come in the form of little pebbles that just aggravate or big rocks that trip us up. Sometimes it will feel like a mountain you can't see over and aren't sure how to get around.

Everyone has their own style of dealing with conflict. Some run and hide, pretending it's not happening. Others will put on their boxing gloves, jump into the ring and be ready to go a few rounds. Some will want to talk about it. Others prefer silence. Some will see it as healthy and inevitable, others as something scary and to be avoided because they've only seen brokenness come from it.

Put a team of people together and conflicts are inevitable and varied. But fall out from conflict – is optional.

Some leaders leave a trail of broken relationships behind them because they have an inability to deal with conflict well. On the other hand, learning to embrace and navigate it is one of the best qualities you can have. How well you deal with it will determine the health of your team and how long leaders choose to stay with you. We had hardly any movement in our leadership team over the eight years we ran youth ministry. A lot of new leaders came and very few left and we think a good part of this was the way we handled conflict.

Back in Adelaide, there were two girls on our team who used to be best friends. Life happened, stuff happened and words were exchanged. It caused a rift that lasted a long time, so long they forgot what they were mad at each other about. Both girls had significant calls of God on their lives. *Sort it out* we said. *But she said this... And she did that... Sort it out* we said again. Their hearts were willing but they were stuck in their hurt and couldn't take that first step. Or one tried while the other stayed where she was. This is where we needed to come in and help because it does matter. We've seen conflict break marriages, split churches and compromise calls. If you can't move forward now, at what stage do you start?

First, you must look inward, do an inventory on how you personally deal with conflict. Cameron is probably the best natural leader in this area but because of my background and childhood, I am more afraid of conflict, preferring for it not to be there, yet the elephant is in the room. For me, conflict meant days of silence and a family so broken, I broke with it. Conflict is scary and personal. Cameron sees conflict as healthy and robust, something that can strengthen and enhance any team. I watch him run toward it with empathy and confidence while I cover my eyes and peer through the cracks waiting for the fall out and am pleasantly surprised when it doesn't come.

Despite your natural bent, you need to make a decision to always deal with conflict. Never let it just sit there because it will be guaranteed to take on a shape and life force of its own which will come back to haunt you, blame and point a finger at you.

When Georgia was a baby I used to go walking with her in the pram. The brand news paths were just being worn in, overshadowed by magnificent gum trees and teaming with bird life. As I strolled around a bend, I came face to face with an Alsatian dog. Being petrified of dogs after having been chased by one as a child, I turned the pram and started running for my life. My fresh caesarean scar was pulling at the sudden activity but I didn't care. I never walked that way again. A lot of us are like that with conflict. We turn and run in panic, but fear is no way to live because I can guarantee you there will be another dog waiting around another corner.

When Cameron passes a dog, he looks it straight in the eye and does not deviate from where he wants to go. He almost challenges it to come at him. This is in the way he handles life. He stares conflict right in the eye, moves toward it and challenges it to even try to ruin that relationship or his day.

We can learn a lot from Cameron. I cannot recall any relationships that have broken down irretrievably in his life, but the few that may have, haven't been because he hasn't tried, but more their unwillingness to play their part. They have turned and run away or stubbornly not been willing to shuffle their way toward him or give even a little.

Cameron operates with the following three things in mind:

Always move toward the person
Don't take it personally
Talk until you understand one another

This pattern has seen him through every situation in good stead all these years. He has the ability to suppress his personal feelings from any situation. It keeps him from reacting out of hurt and striking out with words that once spoken, can never be removed or stuffed back in. He doesn't avoid the person, or walk on the other side of the street. He doesn't ignore their call. No, he purposefully moves toward them. He makes that phone call. He stops and speaks to them in that hallway.

Patiently and calmly, he hears them out. He'll offer his thoughts, but more like a white flag of peace than a cannon of attack. He's not a walkover, but he doesn't give in. He will talk it through, he'll listen, he'll hear. He won't react to blame or words aimed to strike and do damage. He understands and offers perspective. He uses words as a teaching tool, not a punishment and helps them see where he is coming from.

Cameron is the first to say sorry if he needs to and will always accept a sorry if it's offered. He usually ends a conversation with an arm around their shoulder, a hug or a warm slap on the arm, because there is something about genuine physical touch that disarms people quicker and deeper than a thousand words can do.

He's like the conflict coach, encouraging us and anyone on our team to do the same. When he sees or hears of tension between two people, he'll tell them to sort it out. Determined not to breed a culture of whispers behind closed doors, he brings any issues out into the open because dark won't dispel dark, only the light can do that.

ESSENTIAL 25

It's heart before task

We were sitting around the table with a well-loved and experienced youth pastor. Everyone looked up to her. She was one of the pinnacles of youth ministry. Yet she was sitting here, bleeding out over the table, tired and empty of answers. Her youth group had seen a quick decline over the past year and her leadership team had halved. The strain was etched into the corner of her eyes, could be heard in her heavy sigh.

It's not an uncommon problem, when youth ministries have a sudden radical growth that is eventually found to be unsustainable. Teams that were once pulsating with life and energy are left with barely a heartbeat. So they come to us for a diagnosis and prescription.

We look back at the team we served in and then at the team we led a few years later. They were both carried and pushed along with a fierce momentum that seemed never-ending. More volunteers joined and few ever left. So let us offer a few observations we have made, a few pointers on how to keep your teams going over the long haul.

Volunteering truly is a work of the heart. Some teams are driven by events and tasks and to-do lists. They trip over themselves whilst racing from one thing to the next without ever taking time to come up for air. Even discipleship is another meeting, another tick in the 'done' box. Leadership becomes about hustle and bustle, doing and going. This is only sustainable for so long. When people feel they are merely ticking and flicking, getting tasks done, they soon run out of puff. The steam that saw them through one year will not see them through another.

Volunteering is all about heart. It's not about doing but about being. Completing tasks is not the end goal, they are the path to seeing another young life changed. If leaders and volunteers feel their time is spent completing jobs to tick a box, they will soon decide their time is better spent elsewhere. But if they feel that every bit of work they do is changing a life and making a difference, they will be continually re-energised.

One of the motivating factors for us when we served with Russell, was the beautiful equilibrium between serving his vision and in turn feeling as though we were fulfilling our own call. Russell never made the youth ministry about himself. It was us, not me. He always had a very strong direction from God on where we were going in the youth ministry but it was never about *us* making *his* vision happen. Very clearly Russell was the leader but we always knew that we were fulfilling it together. His language was always around us being an army that God had strategically put together to change a generation, that what was happening at that time was special and unusual. So while we busied ourselves with the task at hand, small groups and visitations, prayer meetings and setting up chairs, turning up to band rehearsal and fundraising for camp, we found we were each fulfilling our God-given call. Russell had a way of putting the right people in the right roles, which we can only explain as his prophetic gifting. We weren't plugging holes and meeting random needs because Russell needed us, we were in the right God place at the right God moment for each of our lives.

This one played keys, led worship and wrote songs. That one gathered, pastored and visited. And yet another's crazy creative brain was let loose by buying an old caravan, turning it into a boombox. That has gone down in history as one of our all time favourite memories. We served together for decades because when you are doing what God has called you to do, it gives you grunt and guts and determination. Something powerful happened all those years ago, which we can see God's handprints all over to this day. The smaller parts of our calling were threaded together, woven to create and serve the bigger picture.

Finally, most youth pastors would agree that since leaders are giving so much output, there needs to be input too. They get this part right and wrong all the time. Most will think they are inputting into their leaders, but it's the wrong type. Our friend once put petrol into his Diesel engine. The wrong kind of fuel won't get your leaders far. It's one of the most important principles determining how sustainable your leadership team is. It's the quality of the input that counts. They need regular discipleship where it's not so much about housekeeping and tasks but heart and ministry time.

On top of this, they need you. They don't want another meeting scheduled into their time or a pre-planned mentoring program. They need your lounge-room or to sit across the table from you in a cafe. They want coffee and open hearts and to be asked the hard questions.

In giving so much, they need you to care about them. Not what they do or their role in the youth team. It's the heart stuff. It's the deeper undercurrents of their life that you can only get to by diving in, not by peering at them from a distance.

ESSENTIAL 26

Take a moment to enjoy the wins

You all work so hard. You work and you fight and you give. While others pursue hobbies and leisure activities, you are picking up teenagers and going through Maccas drive-throughs. You spend your money on thick shakes and ice-creams and movies. Sometimes your petrol bill exceeds your weekly earnings. Others pursue lazy mid-morning breakfasts while you are setting up chairs at church. 90% of what you do is the small, the unseen, so the 10% can happen. But it's that 10% that changes lives. Those are the victories, the wins.

We had a win last week. It was *Public* camp. It exceeded our expectations on every level, from Game of G.O.A.T.S (Greatest Of All Time) to dinners of Mexican nachos and chicken schnitzel hamburgers to the friendships that were made. It was the memories of pranking one another by lining their luggage with black rotting bananas. It was hearing the young people sing and watching them worship and feeling their tears as we prayed for them. When we got back to church that Sunday, no-one wanted to say goodbye so they went out for a Chinese dinner together so it would last a few more precious minutes.

It was on the last night of camp that our youth pastor turned to us and said, 'It's been amazing but there's heaps we could do to improve so we'll debrief tomorrow'. We told him *no debrief tomorrow*. Enjoy the win. Celebrate the victory. And they did. With pizza and coke and slaps on the back and one last Chinese meal before school went back.

There will always be more to do and ways to improve but work only, can seep our souls dry. There's nothing more refreshing than being shown everything that's going right, even when a thousand things might be going wrong. We inspire our team when we remind them how amazing they are and how the small wins collectively make a huge difference. Who doesn't like to be part of a winning team? Winning means we've gone long and worked hard together. It means we didn't quit but hustled harder. It means we tried, tried and tried again. We stayed the course, saw it in our heads before we ever held it in our hands.

We understood what true winning is, that it does not lie in the biggest, loudest or fastest but is seen in far more places than that. It's carried in the feet that made their way to the altar to say yes to making Jesus, Lord of their life. It's read in that late night text she wrote, saying 'thank you for praying for me tonight'. It's seen in that small gift, the card with the $30, their little 'thank you' for 'picking me up for youth' every single week. It's felt in the arms of that young person who threw their arms around you at church tonight because they were so very glad to see you.

It's celebrating that song the youth band wrote together and the outreach event you pulled off with hardly any budget. It's looking around and being so grateful you have friends to do life with, to love and laugh with.

It's reminding ourselves to enjoy that last Chinese meal together after Camp Drewe because tomorrow we'll debrief, but for now, there's so much to celebrate.

ESSENTIAL 27

The way to get somewhere is to run in the same direction

An anthropologist proposed a game to the kids in an African tribe. He put a basket full of fruit near a tree and told the kids that whoever got there first won the sweet fruits. When he told them to run they held each other's hands and ran, then sat together enjoying their treats. When he asked them why they had run like that together, as one could have had all the fruits for himself they said: *Ubuntu, how can one of us be happy if all the other ones are sad?* Ubuntu in the Xhasa culture means: *I am because we are.*

Perhaps it is human nature not to want *Ubuntu*. Is it innate within us to push and shove and hustle for the prize, to be seen, to be the best, the winner? Or is this something we have been taught, by living in a culture where it's survival of the fittest and running to get the prize is the ultimate way to live? Have we modelled it, inadvertently rewarded it and therefore created it ourselves? Because if a group of children on the other side of the world have *Ubuntu* as their default, their preferred way of living and being, then perhaps so should we.

We spent the first few weeks observing our leadership team when we took over the youth ministry in Adelaide. There was no linking of arms and running in the same direction. In fact quite the opposite was true. The team were in a flurry of activity, all lone rangers striving to be the hero of the story. It usually involved the stage. There was not a lot of direction and culture-setting from the top and so it was each person for themselves. People were self-appointed in their roles.

This created competition and clashing when two people each decided they were the leader. Most were clambering for the stage, which seemed to be the prized role, the most coveted place to be. So whoever wanted to sing would be on the stage singing and whoever wanted to lead worship would weave their way onto that roster. Preaching was taken in turns to give everyone a go, so there was a whole heap of *look at me, look at me.*

What's interesting about *Ubuntu* is the focus of the prize, the reward at the end being shared. Those children could never be happy, eating and slurping their way through the basket of sweet fruit, if they couldn't share it with others. A prize won alone was not a prize won at all. They had the beautiful and rare mentality that it was only worth something if they could enjoy it together.

Ubuntu is counter-cultural, it's rowing in the opposite direction to the rest of the world, even the Christian world. We tend to reward the seen things: our name on the brochure, that staff position, being chosen to lead worship or share around the next offering message. We feel overlooked if we are only ever asked to do the menial tasks: set up, pack down, canteen, making coffee, visiting that kid, behind the sound desk. The unseen, the small things, therefore have no value. We might feel a little shocked, perhaps offended to see these words on this page. But if we unravel our true motives, scrounge around in the most hidden and deepest parts of ourselves, we find we are all a little guilty. Big numbers at youth, well done, you are a success. More followers on social media, fantastic, you're finally getting noticed. Invited to speak at that conference or church? Phew, I'm finally moving up in the world. Asked to lead worship at youth? Yes, just what I've always wanted.

We take photos of ourselves with 'that person' to show everyone who we're hanging around with. We've made it to the 'green room'. This person has followed me back! Though we say we value the little, the small, the hidden, our actions may just tell the world otherwise.

We knew very early on that one of the values we wanted our youth ministry to be built upon was *Ubuntu*. Every person valued. The prize was not self-gain. The win, the prize, was a leadership team running hand in hand, in the same direction, so we could see the young people in our care find God and purpose and what they were put on this planet for. It was that one gone astray coming back and finding purpose and destiny. It was winning the students in the surrounding schools for Jesus. It was being part of watching a generation fall on their knees discovering what their lives were meant to be. This can only be done if we run together, in the same direction, all in. All for one and one for all!

So we needed to change our actions to match our values. We took everyone's roles away from them and cleared the stage. Since self-promotion on the platform was our biggest issue, nobody was allowed to do anything up front except for us and two of our staff. We starved their appetite for self, sucked the oxygen out of it. At first they didn't like it much, but that was okay with us. It was squeezing what was really on the inside to the outside, like a lemon being twisted and turned to reveal its bitter juices.

We valued the small things, the servant things, like setting up chairs and vacuuming. The least was the greatest in our eyes and we wanted them to see it too. Everybody was required to run a connect group, because this was where the real work happened. The connecting and loving and living with the youth. This is where real life happened and real change would begin. We wanted them to see it wasn't necessarily behind a microphone or on a stage. We were like a huge knitted blanket with a pulled thread, unravelling it back to a messy pile of wool so we could start all over again, weaving and knitting us together in a new way, a better way. Slowly, row by row, we got our team back together, and we were so proud of them as they responded. We pushed, poked and prodded, squeezed and pressed and what began to flow was sweet and fragrant. It smelt of *Ubuntu*. We watched and waited, to find where their gifts lay, who God was on for what. We honoured the one who picked up the vacuum. We lead by example. We developed people for the gifts that they had and taught them that no one was more important or seen or valued more than another.

We never tire of hearing stories like how, decades later, one of our boys who worked the production desk week after week, found his passion and future there. Now he owns a successful production company. Back then, he was the quiet one, the shy one, but the first to arrive and the last to leave. He played his part. He was *Ubuntu* in motion. Another of our girls had a gift for preaching. Her heart was pure and good and sweet so we developed that in her. Decades later, she is a credentialed pastor running a church campus in Sydney with her husband. We could tell you story after story because *Ubuntu does work*. It's something stunning in us that lasts a lifetime. It's a way of living and it's beautiful.

It's not wrong to have ambition and to want to lead or preach or sing. Some people are called to this. But it should never take precedence over other unseen things. It's the motive, it's what lies underneath that counts, as long as we see it as a small part of the overall big picture.

Ubuntu. We need more of this. Imagine entire youth ministries practicing *Ubuntu*. Imagine all of us, in every suburb, in every city, in every state, all around Australia practicing *Ubuntu*. This is our dream. This is our vision. Not one person just a little ahead of the other. Not one person left a little bit behind. Not one person getting all the sweet fruit, all the credit. Not one person striving ahead of another. All of us, running together, hand in hand, as one. This is what will change a generation! *Ubuntu*!

ESSENTIAL 28

Teach team the value of time

hat we would like more than anything else, is to help shape young people who are so proficient at life because this honours God. Doing life well, not perfect, but as well as we can with what we have, is a beautiful thing.

We have a culture in the YA Academy that being on time is being late. Our start time is 9am and so at precisely 9am, we close the door and begin chapel. Anyone who is late, needs to wait in the foyer until chapel is over. That is a 45 minute wait.

The rule came about because it wasn't in our culture and we saw what happened when it wasn't. We learned that what you allow will continue. Everything you do says something about you.

I started to notice that somewhere along the way at the *Academy* we had created a culture that when anyone walked in late, they would be clapped and cheered. Perhaps they thought this would embarrass them into being on time but it didn't work. Instead, it became a college joke. With each passing week more and more people were late and the cheers just got louder. It was really hard to pull things back from there. Even after we set our new rule in place, each week there were two or three who were late.

The group completed the year and with cheers and hurrahs, we handed them their graduation certificates and sent them into the big wide world. One of our students got a job at a high end cafe. He needed this job as he lived by himself and needed the stability of income. Within days of beginning, he rocked up to work late one day. This time there was no clapping, no fun slaps on the back or cheering. Instead he was met with the stern stare of his boss who pulled him aside and told him they had been looking at him as a possible manager. Now he was right back to square one and would need to prove himself again. In fact, they had employed one too many people and because of his tardiness, he might be the one that had to go. This hard truth hit our ex student hard. I felt a little responsible. I knew better. I had a year to teach him some basic essentials for life and I had failed him. It would never happen again.

When our new students arrived, shiny cheeked and eager for the New Year in February, I laid down the law. *You will be on time. The door will shut at 9. If you're not inside, you will sit in the foyer, then you will apologise to the person leading chapel.*

When we are on time, it tells people they matter and their time is important to you. It shows employers you are interested, enthusiastic and organised. It's selfish to be late. It says that you and your time are more important than anyone else's.

We've noticed this pattern emerge in church. Most buildings are almost empty when church begins. On average it takes 15-20 minutes to start to fill up. This is not the kind of people we want to be and it's not the kind of people we want to raise. If there's a leader's meeting, be on time. For church, be on time. When you are interning and have been asked to be there at 1:30, you get there at 1:25. Whether it be your work, youth or uni lectures, be the person who turns up on time. If you tell a parent you'll pick up their young person at a certain time, be there at that time. It says a great deal about you. It tells others that you care about them.

It's real world stuff. When I teach, it's very unprofessional to be driving into school at the same time parents are dropping off their kids. It sends a message that I don't really care or put much effort into my job. The bell goes at a certain time. I like to be there an hour before with all my lessons ready for the day.

The same goes with assignments for study. There is a deadline. Quite a few of our students at the *Academy* fail entire units because they just didn't upload an assessment by 11:55pm. They even look surprised when they are marked zero per cent.

Be on time. Teach your youth team to be on time. Teach your young people the same. You will be doing them a huge favour. They will be a stand out in a world that cares more about itself than others.

ESSENTIAL 29

We all need a Dougie

We've been doing *Youth Alive* for a long time, on our own.

When I say on our own, I mean we've had people, beautiful, solid, good-hearted people around us, but always on loan. The beauty and the difficulty with *Youth Alive* is, everyone is only on loan. Every volunteer comes from another church and we have them on loan for each event. Like borrowing a library book. They don't belong to us permanently. We love them but we eventually have to return them.

Youth Alive is amazing like that because we get to watch the beautiful show of unity as people come together from every denomination and church. It's a haphazard gathering, everyone bringing their unique gift, their talent, their thing, like a potluck dinner. We hardly have time to rehearse and practice, but somehow, whatever we are pulling off, whether a conference or leadership event or *United We Stand*, it ends up looking and sounding like a great masterpiece. We are so proud and so in love with how we, the church, looks and sounds when we come together like that.

There is a downside though and it's behind closed doors. When it's over, everyone returns to where they came from and we are left on our own again. It doesn't mean we don't have friends, because we do. But doing life side by side with a group of friends like we had in Adelaide, we hadn't found the same for the first seven years we lived in Brisbane. That is except for Doug, Dougie Parker.

Cameron discovered him one day from the quiet recesses of Logan, Brisbane. Usually Cameron tells me about someone he's considering employing. That was until Doug. One day he turned up in our study to pick something up. He hardly spoke a word, kind of crept in quietly like he wasn't meant to be there. Cameron's reason for choosing Doug to join our team was that he under-projected and over-delivered on the last high school tour we'd done. That's been the story pretty much ever since with Doug. Under-projected, over- delivered, little talk, much action.

From the first day Doug came to work with us, we've never been alone. We joke that he's the third wheel to Cameron and I, but in all honesty he's the third and the fourth. Because when Doug is around, everything seems to balance, like a wagon with all the wheels aligned correctly so all's right with the world.

Doug sees the best and the worst of us. We can be ridiculously hilarious to work with and sometimes absolutely crazy. Cameron and I banter, have strong discussions and opinions at times and we always try to drag Doug in to agree with one of us, to help us prove our point. But he never takes sides, just smirks and says nothing. Smart man! We drink endless amounts of coffee and talk and talk together. When we talk we can change topics so fast yet we all know what the other is saying.

Within seconds we can change from *Public* to *Youth Alive* to *Academy* and then on to the latest podcast or book we have watched or read.

Doug is our steadying force, our walking source of wisdom. Rarely will we go forward with something unless the three of us agree. Doug will do anything too, even the things he doesn't really like, such as the admin. He's kind, capable and he could run his own thing. Put a microphone in his hand and he will MC or preach. He leads our *Momentum* leadership tours, weaving his way through Regional Queensland with our band. He lectures in the *Academy*, pays the bills, books flights, coordinates every aspect of a conference, *United We Stand* and so much more. He could go and do and be whatever he wants. But he doesn't. Instead he stays with us and drinks copious amounts of coffee.

He's put up with being called the PA and operations manager, when in reality he is so much more. His work ethic is impeccable. There's nothing Doug can't or won't do. Except sing! He can't sing. Well maybe he can, we've just never heard him. But those things are not all he does, as amazing as they are. It's more who he is. He carries our dreams with us and helps fashion the vision. Even though Cameron is the boss, he never pushes his way forward. His humility puts him way up there on a special scale in our eyes. We know we shouldn't do that, but we just can't help it with Doug because he never strives to be there himself.

He knows what he's good at and what he brings and he's content with that. And he has our back. But more than that, his support is sometimes what holds us up when we feel a little weary and undone. Nobody understands the battles we've faced like Doug. The frustrations or sorrows we feel behind closed doors, he is privy to them all. He sees and his constant presence brings back the courage we need to get up and go again.

When Doug decided it was time to move on, to pursue a pastoral role in a church, we were so sad. Well I was sad, because I told Cameron it didn't feel right. I thought he and his family would be with us for longer, like we were all meant to be. But Cameron, as he is so good at doing, always holds people lightly with open hands, so that if they ever need to move on, they can do so. He released Doug with goodwill and love, telling him if ever the day should come that he wanted to return, he could. Besides, we are friends and friends don't just stop being friends. So we prayed and gave him a parting gift as we farewelled him and his family.

About 18 months later, Doug felt that season come to an end. In obedience to God, he resigned. Cameron called and offered him his old job back and eventually Doug said yes. Have you ever seen the movie titled *The Hangover*.[12] It's about a bunch of friends who lose their friend, Doug! They go on a trip together to find him. There's a scene where they are in the car together and one of the guys sings at the top of his lungs 'we're getting Doug back'.

The day Doug decided to come back to us, Cameron went around the house singing that same song the guys from *The Hangover* sang. It showed he was really happy. *We're getting Doug back*. I was so excited that I began to do the same. I kid you not, we did it every day for weeks. Seriously, weeks!

---

[12] *The Hangover, 2009, Legendary Pictures Productions*

We were getting Doug back. Everyone needs a Doug. It could be a guy or a girl, maybe in the form of one person or two or more. We're not talking about a PA, a person to organise your world (although that is very important too). We don't mean a colleague or staff member or someone who clocks in at eight and clocks off at five. We're talking about a Doug. The person who gets you and gets what's in your heart. The person who makes you get out of bed in the morning and press on when it's hard and messy and complicated. The one who sees what you see when you can't explain it in words. They will carry what you carry and even take over when it gets too heavy for you. They answer your crazy 11pm calls and cover your weaknesses. They pick up when you drop things, because they get all the plates you are spinning. You work hard together and always side by side. When you have a win you celebrate, side by side, even sit back for a second and smile because it's really worth it.

Then you move onward and upward to the next thing, because there is always a next thing. When days turn into months and months into years, you look back and realise that they were always there right next to you. Ploughing the ground, sowing seeds, watering, waiting, watching something grow, and even if they're not there forever, you are so grateful for walking the path together for a while.

So Dougie, thank you. Thanks for being you. Thank you for being with us, alongside us, creating paths where there were none and always saying yes to the next adventure. If the day comes, when we ever have to part ways again, even though we never want to, well we won't ever say goodbye. Because we'll be friends forever, or in the words of Winnie the Pooh, *even longer.*

ESSENTIAL 30

Don't forget the elephant in the room

We'd almost finished writing this book when a particular issue came up, a warning sign begging to be aired. We could no longer ignore it. It's probably one of the most common yet damaging issues happening amongst young people and unfortunately, in youth leadership teams.

So we couldn't close the final page without addressing this because it's perhaps one of the most important things we can say.

It will never ever be out of fashion to strive to live Holy lives, according to God's principles.

So, we need to discuss this sometimes delicate issue. Sex outside of a committed married relationship is clearly out of bounds according to Scripture.

In the past few years, we've had it come to our attention more than ever that it's no longer the exception for those in key youth positions to be compromising about this. It's become a problem amongst entire youth teams. What is even more worrying is the amount of youth pastors and senior pastors that know about it but turn a blind eye. The reason is they don't want to have to step that person down or deal with it because they think they need that person on their team.

I don't know of any parent who wants their teenage son or daughter sleeping around and youth groups should always be considered a safe place for their kids to attend. Therefore when it's being ignored as happening on the youth team, it eats away at the leader's authority and credibility to even talk about it with young people. The thing is that the standards we allow for our youth are the standards that will permeate the entire group.

Youth ministry is an important vehicle for reinforcement of Christian values and God's clear principles from His Word. Any breach of these values or God's principles needs to be nipped in the bud quickly.

We were travelling together in the car a few weeks ago discussing this issue. Our own youth group is not exempt. Where there's a group of people, there is opportunity for this issue to arise. We agreed that we need to keep setting a high standard in this area for youth groups across the country. We can do it by showing the hows and whys with continuing follow up, especially with the leaders. Together we can lift the standards and facilitate our youth and youth leaders back into living God's way. It's the only true path to freedom.

We've had to call this issue out on two separate occasions. The response from these two people were as different as night from day, hot from cold, fire from ice. One cast blame and fury, the other invited correction and restoration. The first caught our breath for a second, but it made us more resolute about our values. They are to be lived and led according to God's word. If that makes us the bad guys, then so be it. One day we will stand before the Lord to give account for every young person that was in our care and if that means standing up time and time again for God's standards and demanding the same in our teams, then that is what we will keep fighting for.

What you allow will continue

If we allow young people to sleep around in our leadership team then it can potentially happen amongst our youth. The culture we set from the top is the culture that will permeate through your entire youth ministry.

We hear about too many leaders throwing their hands up in defeat, as though they can't do anything about it in 'this day and age'. This is an excuse and weak leadership. We need to set the tone. We need to set the standard. We are the leaders and we are the examples for our teams to follow. So lead by example.

With this in mind, anytime it comes to our attention, we call it out. We humbly and gently go to the people involved and have one of those hard but life altering conversations.

Our heart is always to restore

We call it out not to judge, not to tell somebody off, not to catch them out, but to see them restored. When two people sleep together outside of marriage, they leave a little piece of themself behind. It rarely ends well. Feelings get hurt. Friendships are irreparably damaged. Future marriages are torn before they even begin.

Whatever God has put in His word, is for our own good. A rule becomes our freedom. A boundary stops us from careering over the edge. A red light stops us from becoming a wreck.

The pathway to restoration

When you confront somebody about having sex outside of marriage, it's a good idea to give them a break from leadership responsibilities. It's not to punish them but to give them time out to reflect, to spend time with God and be returned and restored back onto His path for their lives.

It also sets an unwavering standard and sends a message to the rest of the team. It's better than any sermon on the subject. It reminds everybody what you value – and what you value is living according to God's word.

We would suggest perhaps three months as a guide but each situation is different.

Put the person before the youth ministry

A senior pastor actually said they turned a blind eye because they needed that person's skill. They couldn't call them out, step them down for a while, because then who would lead worship or lead that team?

What have we become when our ministry means more to us than a person who needs help? Have we become so competitive, bought so much into the lie of being the biggest and the best that we are willing to turn a blind eye to save ourselves?

God honours holiness. God honours a leader who loves a person enough to help restore them even if it means their ministry goes without for a while. And we have always found that God provides another person to fill in, just in time!

The enemy will do everything to push people together before they are married and then do anything to pull them apart after.

These words expose the exact plan of the enemy. In whiney, excusing voices, young people will say it's just too hard. Don't accept that excuse. They can do it. We did it. God never puts anything in His word that is unachievable.

Living according to God's word is a decision and we need to teach young people to choose God every day and in every area of their lives.

Just because something is common doesn't make it right and even though it's done en masse it doesn't mean it's good for us.

God's standards are normal. Not having sex before marriage is normal. Entire youth leadership teams committed to waiting until marriage is normal.

God is looking for a generation willing to live according to his Holy plan and principles. The moral standard of the world might be crumbling little by little, but our God is the same yesterday, today and forever. A youth pastor who fights to keep God's standards will reap the rewards for sure!

PART 3
TRANSFORMING YOUTH MINISTRIES

ESSENTIAL 31

Build according to God's blueprint

When you create according to the pattern that God has given you, it is a little like being a clothes designer, creating a design that's never been done before. If you stay on the path that He has laid for you, and it's clear it has never been trodden before, you are following His blueprint. When nobody can tell you what's around the next bend or how far the road stretches or what's over the next hill, you are living by a blueprint.

If you cannot find a list of rules, do's or don'ts or podcasts to help you with your next step, you, my friend, are on an adventure all your very own. Well done you! For this will be the very best of adventures.

When you look back and see the result of being obedient to each little pattern God puts before you, well that is how blueprints are made. It takes a good deal of guts and grit to live this way. In fact, it takes lashings of it. God doesn't show you the whole big picture before you begin. He reveals it in little snippets at a time. The human psyche wants more information before we commence something new and untried.

We want reassurance, a nod and wink that everything will work out fine. But this is not life, at least not life in the Faith lane.

According to the Collins English Dictionary (2012 digital edition), *a blueprint is an original plan or prototype that influences subsequent design or practice.*

We have the blueprints for our house. It was built in 1979, the builder was an architect and also owner of the house. Rolled up and kept in a tube, every now and then we open it, like an historical scroll. On this paper are the dreams of one man, a blueprint before one brick was ever laid. There's no house exactly like it. Today you can go to any display village, fall in love with one of their designs and say *I'll have one like this please* and that's lovely. But there's a hundred other people like you, who will fall in love with the same house design and say *I'll have one just like this please.* You can drive into any new housing estate, all brand new houses and see a dozen that look the same, built to the very same plan.

This is the very reason we love our house. There is nothing else quite like it. The cathedral ceilings are majestic and we practically live in the treetops. We have a skylight that the crows pick at incessantly in the spring and a cute little dining room that is poky and homey all at the same time. It has nooks and crannies and a gazillion places to nestle in. The indoor/outdoor flow is not brilliant and one of the trees has been planted way too close to the house. It's odd and lovely but original. When we wanted to refinance our home loan, the evaluator oohed and ahhed over it and questioned why anyone would ever want to sell such a lovely home. It's not perfect and we get frustrated with the upkeep at times, but it's got so much going for it. We've raised our babies here, so we just can't give it up. Memories have soaked into the walls and foundations that now belong to us.

This is how we see our life with God, a 'never been designed before' blueprint. It's the lens through which we see *Youth Alive* and *Public* and the *Academy*. When we have the privilege of being handed a task, a calling by God, we are so very honoured that we couldn't make it look like everyone else's. Our creative, wild and thoughtful God is absolutely original in everything He creates and He gives us license to do the same. Every new born baby we have ever held looks completely different. No two babies are the same. No two people are the same. No two callings are exactly the same.

Going back to when we first took over *Solid Rock*, God told us to bring His presence back and we knew it was our own blueprint. It was the plan of action, the outline, which would influence our practice and every decision we made in the youth ministry. It was like seeing an overview, a picture from a distance. We could make out the basic design easily enough, but the detail was fuzzy. That part we did a little at a time. We scheduled a camp for later that year. No guest, no hype, it was to be 'in house', which meant we were to be the speakers. The weekly program was centred around worship and a Word and then a response to the Word. There was nothing flashy to draw the kids in. No big give-aways. No big plans to woo them. Just us, God, an Altar and stopping the buses for a while.

The other thing we did, which turned out to be one of the keys at that time, was discipleship with our leaders (which we have spoken about in a previous essential). There were about 25 of them at the time. They were friends and we threw open the doors of our house every fortnight.

It was compulsory for them to come to discipleship and waiting for them was a different kind of altar. It was the altar of our lounge room floor. We didn't talk about admin or strategy or program. We didn't do a study, or a topic. We talked. We brought a word, not one written by someone else, but one written on our hearts. We wrote it on theirs.

We all shared. Our fears, our insecurities, how it felt the day our dad walked out, the struggle of our faith, watching our mum battling cancer. The way we felt we didn't fit or we were too loud or too quiet. We prayed over them. We held hands. Then we ate pizza, like it was some sort of healing balm for our soul, and on special nights we made them pancakes because Cam and Renee cooking for them was next level!

Our door was open during the week too. Sometimes they would fall in, sprawl on our couch and tell us of thwarted love or a secret sin. We came undone together. We were brought back up, together. We became family. Our stories were like a random box of ribbons, intertwined and muddled up in the most beautiful way. As Cam and I did life well together, that was transferred to the young people. Suddenly we weren't just doing a job together, we were changing lives.

When we prayed for the young people at the altar, our hearts were kneaded with theirs. We loved them fiercely. God's heart beat in our chest for them. We clung to them and walked with them through life. Not just the beautiful places like the altar, but on their Mondays and Tuesdays too. The more we fell in love with God and them, the more they did too.

100 kids grew to 200, then 300 and more. The leadership team grew until we could no longer fit into our lounge. They were our most favourite of days. What God did, as we followed His blueprint, was to

build the loveliest of all designs. Not a program, but a bunch of young people who became family together.

So go ahead! Open your ears and be bold and brave enough to ask God for a blueprint all your own!

ESSENTIAL 32

Dig down before you build up

What we are about to tell you is counter cultural and will take guts and courage to outwork. In a time where it's all about being seen, measuring success in numbers and promoting self, we will tell you the opposite. Time and again, Jesus walked away from the very same patterns the world promotes today. He walked away from compare and compete, from elevating oneself in order to be seen. He was all about humility and serving as keys to the most powerful leadership on the planet.

Sometimes it's hard to tell if people are building a youth ministry, young people or their own brand. Priorities seem to have gone belly up. The building of a big youth ministry is a quick ticket to being recognised and invited to preach in other places. We all need to check ourselves and investigate our motives. Inevitably, if what we are doing is working in our youth ministry and we are seeing 'success' it is natural for the invitations to come our way. In some cases, people are promoting and branding themselves, even paying for sponsored ads on social media. We need to care less about the platform and more about the foundations we are building for our young people and the fruit we see in their lives. Grow fruit over building platforms. Dig down before you build up.

Platforms are usually all about me. They are a stage to show myself off to the world. It's about marketing and strategy, filling our feeds with pictures of ourselves preaching and who we are with, veiled thinly under the guise of love for young people. Everyone wants to be part of something big, as long as they are the boss. They are happy for unity, as long as they are the one owning that unity.

We do need a platform, we need someone to lead and a place to lead from. But this generation deserves platforms with good, supporting foundations. They need a platform that is for their good over our ego. The substance of our platform lies in the strength of our foundations and good ones simply cannot be built without doing the hard work. The best youth leaders are found in the dark, in the hidden, digging deep in the trenches. It is these same leaders who are the most ready and deserving of any platform that arises. Grow good fruit, build a solid foundation and you will have something worth saying when you are on the platform.

Let's do a comparison between platform and foundation:

PLATFORM

a. Platforms elevate the one 'up there' while everyone else comes to watch and marvel. It puts value on self and being noticed. It teaches young people that value comes from a platform.

b. Platforms are about entertainment and attracting a crowd. Some youth ministries are built on hype, give-aways, great social media and anything they can think of to attract a crowd. There is nothing wrong with a crowd, but if there are no foundations being built, then gathering a crowd is nothing more than presenting a picture of success. Egos may be built but what about hearts?

c.   Platforms are all about accolades and applause. Satan tempted Jesus to become spectacular. The sound of applause wrecks youth pastors all the time. We cannot lean into applause because it cannot sustain us.

d.   Platforms are a hungry beast that needs constant feeding. We get some success, so we want more. We get a preaching gig somewhere, so we want another. Again, they feed our egos but do nothing to feed our young people.

e.   Platforms build a following but it is a shallow following without a strong foundation. Young people will go with the crowd and the latest thing, so they will only follow for a while. They will not follow what has not captured their heart and is transforming them in the process.

FOUNDATIONS

a.   Foundations are built in the hidden recess of the underground, the places not noticed. They are not usually Instagram worthy. It's the car pick-ups and drop-offs and the beautiful conversations that happen in the in-between. It's the being there, sitting with them in the dark sometimes. It's putting out chairs, setting up hang-zones and making the 100th call for the week. We dig in a million different ways and the results cannot be measured straight away. It's the digging in the dark, with no applause, where we really begin to take ground.

b. Foundations can't be done by one. While a platform can be easily occupied by one, it takes a team, an 'us' to dig deep. It's the pulling in the same direction, the 'we're in this together' culture. It's the spaces and places where memories are made and team become family. *Youth Alive* is like this, we look around us and see Doug and Shani and Brad. Sweating and ploughing shoulder to shoulder are Ben and Emily. It's sharing the load, all the while knowing we are doing it to change lives.

c. Foundation takes patience and time. When all you want to do is build up, create something amazing that can be seen and applauded, it can feel frustrating to be doing something in the opposite direction. You are going down into the hidden instead of up into the view of others. You find yourself turning dirt instead of stacking bricks. But don't give up, don't rush the process because the deeper you go, the stronger and better the building will be. Without digging deep, there will be no lasting legacy. Take time to create that healthy culture in your team. Be patient with those leaders. Catch up with them again and again. Have the hard conversations. Insist on pastoral care being a value in your youth. Build a worship team who are about presence and not performance.

d. Foundations are about doing the boring work over and over but eventually it yields a ton of fruit. If only all of us will just do the little things, the boring things, consistently. It's like eating the right thing again and again. Exercising day in, day out. It's the boring things that bring the spectacular results. Year after year, we have spent our time doing the mundane in youth ministry and *Youth Alive*. We work hard, we work long and slowly, and after 10 years of being in *YA*, we see conferences in nearly every state, 30,000 young people gather for *UWS*, but that has come from digging deep consistently.

We see a generation of youth pastors and leaders rising, who are willing to do the behind the scenes, the boring stuff. The bits that are not sexy, but necessary. The future of our Australian youth will be built by them. They understand that in order to go high, one must first go deep. They know we need to embrace the process for the best final results. Their motive is not for themselves but for our young people to fully live their God purpose. How can we build strong foundations when we are too busy building our own platforms? Young people don't need our platforms, they need our hands and our hearts.

ESSENTIAL 33

Great youth ministries are built over time

When I was about 10 years old, my sister, my cousin and I went to stay with my dad like we usually did in the school holidays. He lived on the North Shores of Sydney and behind his house, if you climbed far enough down into the gully, was a little body of water that fed into the harbour. We were bored one day, so my dad happily agreed for us to go play on our own by the water. It was the 80's and this was what kids did back then. We soon grew tired of being by the water so we thought it would be far more adventurous to be on the water, so we decided to build a raft.

I have no idea where we got the wood from, but somehow we gathered some long pieces and tied them together with rope, which my cousin snuck out of a shed that was down the back of my Dad's house. We had so much faith in our little raft that had taken all of 20 minutes to build, and with sticks for oars, hopped on board our masterpiece and pushed off into the great unknown which was all of a few metres to the other side. About half-way to our destination, the raft started tilting on a weird angle and the wood that seemed so secure on land started to drift apart as the rope slackened. With lightning speed we made our way back to the water's edge, and back onto dry land, just in time before our raft fell apart. We laughed as we caught our breath, no one wanting to admit to the other how our hearts were now lodged in our throat instead of in our chest, where they belonged. I don't know if my dad ever figured out what we had done that day, but he never asked so we never told.

There was something my 10 year old self didn't know back then, which is quite clear to me now. Good things are built over time, nothing worth building is easy and there is always fruit if you wait around long enough to see.

It's easier and far more convenient to build something in a flash. It's more satisfying in the moment to build something you can jump on straight away and yell look at me, look at me! Isn't this thing I made so amazing! But the thing with quick and easy is, it never seems to build anything that truly lasts.

It's so much easier and much more convenient to slap a few sticks together, throw a random rope around them, cross our fingers and toes and hope it will hold us. But in truth, building something strong and worthwhile takes time and it's very rarely easy.

This particular year, we had returned from our third *Youth Alive* conference that year. This one was in our hometown in South Australia. For us this was where our story began – our life story, our God story. It is here we heard God's voice and answered Him with a resounding yes. Queensland might be home now but Adelaide will always have a piece of our heart. It's the place where we became who we are. We have friendships there that stretch over decades. We never thought we'd be old enough to say that, but here we are. We know people who have been friends longer than the time we spent in school.

Surrounding us that week, at every turn, were familiar faces. They were the faces of the teenage children of some of our best friends. They were the faces of the young people whose parents were teenagers in our early youth ministry. We were floored at how fast time goes by. Most of these young ones call us 'Uncle Cam' and 'Aunty Reneè' because although we are not real family, when you do life together like we have with their parents, you have earned the right to be called family. Others heard their squeals of recognition and turned and stared and wondered.

Deep down in my soul, I absolutely loved it. These young people had the right to call us Aunty and Uncle because we had shared so much of life with their parents. We have had the beautiful honour of watching what happens when something is built slowly over time. We were not building a church or a youth ministry together all those years ago. We were building people and lives and memories. We didn't worry that it didn't happen overnight. We weren't in a rush to put something together to make ourselves look important and good or like we were achieving. None of that mattered. Though God might never call you to stay in one area of ministry for a long time, like we have with *Youth Alive*, let us assure you that when you take your time and build well, the results will take your breath away.

Two of the boys were the sons of dear friends. When they went into labour with their first son, they called us, in the middle of the night. We bolted down to the hospital and sat with them for a while, laughing and talking and marvelling that they were about to bring a tiny human into the world. They let us in at the most sacred time in their life.

Cameron and our friend were on staff together, and nothing broke our hearts more than when a few years later, their marriage unravelled and they parted ways. Now that tiny human is a strapping 19 year old and his brother is 17. But despite what they have been through, to see how much they loved Jesus and how pure and good their hearts are was a memory that will burn in our hearts forever from that week.

Then there was Amy, a troubled teenager who was in our life group all those years ago. She pushed God and people away, but we kept chipping away at her and loving her and showing her Jesus. We would visit and call and show up at her house. All these years later, in the carpark at conference, she showed up. She threw her arms around us and held on for dear life, a silent thank you. She told us that she had been dropping her own kids, now teenagers, at conference all week. Later she wrote on our Instagram the loveliest of words that we want to frame, a reminder to never give up and never think that seeds sown can't grow into something precious.

Mentors and leaders I knew as a teenager are now speaking into my teenagers' lives. Never underestimate the power of your words and actions. They have certainly impacted our lives in so many ways and we cherish them to this day.

There are many others that we can tell you about. We hold them all close, like they belonged to us. We feel like they really do. They are a part of our heart, our history, the reason we get up everyday and get on planes and keep showing up. Because we've seen something and we want them to know it too. Good things, beautiful things, like hearts, are built over time. It's not about life, right now. Every seed sown is not going to give a return straight away. The return could be a decade from now. It could be returned in the lives of their future children. Do you get that? Seeds that you sow now, can actually be impacting not just this generation but the generations to come. They take time, care and attention and require us to keep on showing up. It's not about slapping something together to get quick results.

We've seen the truth that anything worth building takes time and lots of it. You can't hurry it. There's no quick fix, no easy way around. But there will always be fruit, if you wait around long enough to see it.

Though it was fun on our raft in the creek that day, let me remind you what my 10 year old self didn't know and what my adult self still at times needs reminding of – that good things take time. However, we are building lives, not rafts, and we might not see the results straight away. Every car pick up you do, each conversation, every time you sit with them and each lesson you prepare for life group, you're not just trying to help them make it a few metres to the other side. You are building support and strength and a strong foundation so they can make it across to the other side of life, in rough or calm seas. We must do this with the next generation in mind and the next. I know it now. I have seen and I understand.

ESSENTIAL 34

Teach leaders and youth to pray mountain moving prayers

This generation is not any ordinary group of young people. Even with mobile phones and Adidas shoes, they are not the hopeless ones. They are warriors, and their prayers can move mountains. But do they know? Do we tell them? Do we put down our phones, clear our busy schedules, get on our knees and pray? Do we clear our calendar, shift our appointments and provide them with opportunity?

We were given a great gift growing up in our church in Adelaide. We were shown how to pray. We were encouraged to pray. We were given regular opportunities to pray. We can still hear it, feel it, see it. Groups, rooms full of young leaders and young people, brushing past one another, walking up and down in rows like busy ants in their colony. Without fear or hesitation or wondering how we sounded, we cried out to God, our voices raised in a joint war cry, a battle song. We prayed like this before every meeting.

We prayed like this every Wednesday morning at 6.30am, hands warming in our pockets, but praying none-the-less. We didn't do this for a few months or a few years, we did it for decades, together in the upstairs room at our church. It was fighting in the trenches, waging a war on an unseen enemy. Is it any wonder that some of the greatest pastors and leaders we see in our country and beyond, came out of that church and from those days. Is it any wonder that *Planetshakers*, a global phenomenon, was birthed there?

Now God wants to do it again. He is not a God that looks back nostalgically on yesterday. He is a God who wants to do it again. He can and He will. It's up to us to teach the next generation. They have to know that their prayers can move mountains.

Making prayer a priority is a necessity. We need to schedule prayer meetings regularly and a great place to start is before youth. Set a time, about an hour or so before and require every leader and volunteer to be there. Encourage young people to come. When they come, teach them how to pray – really pray. There is a place and time for quiet, reflective prayer. This kind of prayer is beautiful and fragile and soul-altering. But there's another kind of prayer, the kind that sounds like faith and authority and fervour. The Bible says that the 'fervent' prayers of a righteous man or woman, makes a lot of power available.

Fervent means with zeal. Zeal means 'with great energy or enthusiasm in pursuit of a cause or an objective.'

When we are at a sporting event, barracking for a team, we get loud and enthusiastic. We do it with great energy and noise. When many voices join together, it creates an electric atmosphere in that arena. This is true for prayer. Yet it's becoming common for us to walk into prayer meetings and not hear anyone pray. Everyone is standing still, in their own little corner, whispering something perhaps self-consciously. This is not the kind of prayer this verse is talking about. When we are excited about a conversation we are having with somebody, we are animated and energetic. This is what we need to teach our young people about prayer. Enthusiastic, energetic, zealous prayer holds a great deal of power. Done together, it creates an incredible atmosphere of faith. Teach them not to be afraid of their own voice. Pray and believe for great things together and point out when God answers. Build their faith, one prayer at a time, brick upon brick.

Remind them that their words are not floating on some invisible cloud, or disintegrating into the atmosphere. Their words are reaching the ears of God, the 'I can do anything' and 'nothing is impossible' God. When God made Adam and Eve, he put them in charge of the earth and all that was in it. We still hold that authority today. God needs us to partner with Him, in prayer, to bring His purposes to pass right in front of them. Pray for their schools. Pray for salvation for their friends. Pray for the youth ministry. Pray for themselves and their families. Believe for answers to their 'we can't do this on our own' kind of prayers.

We were so impacted by a story that Phil Pringle[13] told last year when he was at our leadership event. He was standing at the window praying and praising, when he heard a strange noise. He thought it was the air conditioner in the hotel, so he continued to pray. The noise was getting louder and seemed close. As he turned slightly to look behind him, he saw the corner of an angel wing, filling the room. As he praised, the

---

[13] *Phil Pringle founded C3 Church Global in 1980, now a movement of 500+ churches in 60 countries*

angel wing was being fueled to move faster. He was in complete awe, standing on Holy ground, with an angel present right there with him.

We need to tell our young people stories like this – because they are not just stories, they are reality. Our young people have the power of God within them and are called to do great things for God. They have angels watching over them, holding and protecting them in all their service and obedience. The God of the universe listens to them. He is super interested in what they have to say. Their prayers are the things miracles are made of. They can change worlds and atmospheres and lives with their prayers. The soles of their feet are called to walk into battle zones and their mouths open uttering prayers as they go.

This is why we say no phones at youth. How can they hear God when they are distracted by texts and social media? We need young people more taken with the throne than their phone, ready to fall on their knees, open their mouths and pray. This is why we say 'stand up' when we worship and listen when we talk. It's training them to listen out for God, to make room for Him. We should put more value on a young person turning up to a prayer meeting than anything else. A young person with a microphone is just that – one person. But a group of young people with their voices going heavenward, no stage, no microphone, no spotlight, now that is the something that miracles are made of.

Youth groups will see revival because of prayer. This nation will see a revival because of prayer. Schools will see a revival because of prayer. The Bible is clear in 2 Chronicles 7:14 NIV that if we humble ourselves and pray and seek His face and pray and turn from our sins and pray, God will heal our land. It won't be through a preaching gift, as good as that is. It won't be a conference or an event. God wants us to humble ourselves and come to Him in prayer.

Young people will begin to heal – from confusion, loneliness and fear; from anxiety, depression and self-harm; rejection, anger and despair; bullying, selfishness and insecurity. Think about this on a big scale – most youth groups meet on a Friday night. Imagine the sound in heaven as tens of thousands of young people, in thousands of youth groups, in every city and every country town praying from school halls, youth halls, gym halls and basketball courts. From living rooms, side rooms and everywhere else that youth ministries meet around the nation. Imagine the angel's wings, fueled by their voices. Swishing and swooshing; faster and louder. The power that would come down from Heaven then!

ESSENTIAL 35

Lead this generation to the cross

Nearly 20 years ago, *Rich Wilkerson Snr[14]* preached a message that still echoes through the years and reaches us today. It was one of those sermons that has gone down in history as being far more than just a message. It's a mantra, life changing words to any generation. It was titled *'I Want the Cross'*. He spoke of putting down the things in our hands and picking up the Cross. During the sermon, he lugged a huge, bulky, wooden cross on his back. The imagery burned our eyes and reached our souls. The room was thick with conviction.

At the end, Rich had us all on our knees, weighing up the cost and inconvenience of saying yes to the call. Then, if we wanted, if we were ready and if we meant it, he asked us to stand up and shout at the top of our voice 'I WANT THE CROSS.' The room was silent at first, heavy with awe. We knew it was a holy moment, a set apart moment, one we would remember for the rest of our lives. A moment that divided life into two parts – before and after we said 'yes' to the Cross. Most

---

[14] *Rich Wilkerson Snr is a prominent evangelist and author who founded Peacemakers and Peacemakers Family Centre*

of us in that room already loved Jesus with our whole being. We also believed in defining moments such as this. We have been so incredibly blessed that way. We grew up in a church, a youth group, where a few defining moments shaped who we are today – a night, a meeting, a moment, where the ordinary collided with the extra-ordinary, the natural with the supernatural, the human with the divine. This was one of those times.

One shaking, brave voice spoke, I WANT THE CROSS. Then a second, I WANT THE CROSS, a third and fourth followed at the same time. Voices echoed and crossed over one another. I WANT THE CROSS. Pride was put aside. Selfish ambition laid down. Agendas came apart with those words – I WANT THE CROSS. Hundreds, thousands of voices shouted their commitment that night. Our voices became the music, each seat an altar. 20 years later we can still hear those voices echo.

In the room that night were young men and women who have gone on to do incredible things for God. Some of the best leaders around Australia and the world now, were in the building that night. Some are leading churches of hundreds, thousands and tens of thousands. Some have written Grammy award winning music. Some have begun movements, preached on stages in front of hundreds of thousands of people, began conferences, written books.

It is time for another generation to cry I WANT THE CROSS. It's time for a new army of young people to buckle at the knees, fall under the weight of His Call. Are things different from 20 years ago? Perhaps! We have presented a Gospel that is so entertaining. We have the lights and show, the social media and the give-aways. We know how to pull all the punches to get young people walking through those doors. We make it all easy, attractive and convenient, feeding them and burping them so they can be as comfortable as possible. But the Cross! The beautiful, blessed, raw and rugged Cross is not convenient or comfortable. The Cross is counter cultural. It's a die so you can live, lose your life to find it, get on your knees if you want to go up culture. Serve if you want to be great. Be the last. Be the least. Forgive. We tell these young people to take risks while protecting them and wrapping them in processes and procedures to minimise any risk. We tell them they can do anything while we do everything for them. We tell them to take up their Cross when they struggle to put down their phone.

It's up to us. We have to lead the way, show them and inspire them. God wants to capture their hearts and encounter this generation. His eyes are roaming the earth, looking for the young one on their knees, paying the price, putting aside convenience and comfort, wanting Him more than anything else in their life. We're telling you, young people want something to live for. The ones coming through are some of the most selfless young people we have seen. They understand what is happening in this world around them. They want to help, they want to make a difference and give their life for a cause. So we need to remind them who they are and help them rise up to be all they were put on this earth to be. It's like refusing to be the parent who only gives their kids sour straps and starburst lollies. We know they are made to experience more than that which tastes good.

We need to tell them stories of people who have gone before and given their all. Create opportunities for them to encounter God, fall in love with Him and hear His voice. Teach them to bring their Bible, an actual Bible – a hard copy, not an app – and a pen and notebook. They need to listen and learn and write notes and discover the whispers of God for themselves threaded through their journal entries. They need to turn on worship in their bedrooms, on a Monday and Tuesday and Wednesday and lift their hands and sing from their very soul.

We can see a generation who don't want to just observe a revolution but be the revolution in their schools, where the little things matter like getting up and getting to school on time, trying their best and being kind, fierce and brave. We need young people whose integrity is fierce and who don't stay between the lines, because God loves young people who spill out of the box.

God's after young people who value thy will, not my will. Who ask *what do you want for my life* rather than *what do I want?* Youth willing to let God breathe on their careers and be the centre of their dating life. Who have the word You on their lips more than Me. Who can see past today and dream huge, God dreams about tomorrow, who don't mind being inconvenienced and uncomfortable. It's a new breed God is looking for. We had a prophetic word just a few months ago that God was raising up a new breed of young people in Australia and they would line up in their dozens, then hundreds and then thousands.

So let's take their hand and show the way. Tell them stories as we walk a while, inspire them and tell them to dream. Speak life and prophesy over them. Provide moments for them to encounter God at youth and small groups. Take them to camps and conferences where they are in bigger environments. Position them whenever and wherever you can so they can encounter God like we did.

May this generation not conform, may they not be tamed. May they shout, no roar those words – I WANT THE CROSS – so they can be heard by the generations to come.

ESSENTIAL 36

Create strong atmospheres intentionally

I read somewhere that an atmosphere is the pervading tone or mood of a place. Whether you realise it or not, your youth ministry has a certain atmosphere about it. You carry an atmosphere with you. The question is, is it an accidental one or are you setting a tone and mood intentionally?

From the moment parents drive into your car park, there is a tone and mood that says everything about you. We must own and value everything from the car park to the toilets.

Years ago we were sitting in the fourth row in a church meeting. Week after week we found ourselves wanting to leave even before the last song was played. A quick get away was a relief. So we talked about what was driving us away instead of connecting us into that place and decided the atmosphere played a big role. When we prayed for needs, people mumbled quietly under their breath and we remember thinking how if ever we were desperate for prayer, this would be the last place we would raise our hands and ask. The people on the stage were often new and inexperienced, which left us feeling nervous for them. There was no sense of faith and wonder that God could do anything, right there, in that moment.

Even during worship the lights were left burning chasms into our eyes as everybody else was obviously looking around instead of engaging. Even during announcements, the music behind the MC was too loud or too soft or droning in some minor key. Like how Goldilocks would have felt, everything was much too big or much too small and it didn't feel like home.

We must have attention to detail in every area of our youth meeting. Young people are especially sensitive to atmospheres. They love a good one and won't come back if it's not there. Imagine yourself being new or a young person walking into your youth ministry. This has nothing to do with hype and everything to do with making sure your young people want to come back.

Below are questions to ask yourself, a bit of a self quiz to measure what kind of atmosphere your youth group is setting, from the moment they drive in to the venue to the last goodbye:

WALKING IN

What experience are the parents having in the carpark when they drop their teenager off?
Do we welcome the young people in a way that makes them feel immediately comfortable?
Is there energy and care in an authentic way?
Do we make sure nobody is on their own, outcast and isolated?

AESTHETICS

What are the aesthetics of our building like?

Is it a warm, friendly place to be?

Is our music good (not too loud but not too soft)?

Is it intimidating to walk into our youth building?

Have we created a good mood with low lighting and smaller spaces for youth to be with each other?

Are the toilets clean and smell good?

Have we made a larger space feel smaller and intimate?

MEETING

Have we got the right number of seats out? Empty seats can suck faith right out of the building!

Do we allow youth to sit down at the back and not be engaged?

Are our front few rows filled with energetic young people and leaders who lead by example and set the tone?

Do we pull everyone forward in a tight group, which creates a great atmosphere to engage during worship?

Has our worship team chosen good songs that everyone is familiar with?

Do they introduce one new song at a time and sandwich it in between ones they know?

What are the transitions between songs like?

Are our young people engaged in worship and if not what can we do to change this?

Does the worship leader read the crowd to see what keeps them engaged and what loses them?

Are the lights down so they can worship freely without feeling like everyone is watching them?

Are the leaders scattered around the young people, leading by their presence?

When young people open their Bibles is there excitement and a sense of value in the word?

Do young people engage and take notes or are they flicking through social media?

Who are we allowing to have a go on the stage?

Do they engage the youth? Do they have believable authority?

What kind of behaviour dominates in the crowd?

Are we setting that tone or are they?

Are you creating an atmosphere of faith where young people are expectant and excited, eagerly leaning in to what God can and might do?

Do our words create a sense of expectation that God is right here and wants to do something in their lives tonight?

Do they agree and encourage the preacher or are they bored and silent?

During an altar call, do leaders come down and stand with the youth straight away?

Do they pray over them with authority or do they mumble prayers that show a lack of confidence?

When the meeting finishes, is there awkward silence for a moment before the music starts to play?

AFTER THE MEETING

Is there an atmosphere of family and connection?

Is anyone left on their own?

Is everyone being included?

What will they tell their parents when they ask 'how was youth'?

There are so many details that create good or poor atmospheres. Your youth ministry has an atmosphere already but it is up to you to dictate what kind it is and encourage the youth to join with you in upping the ante.

The best atmosphere setters are you and your leaders. Atmospheres must be lead and created intentionally. Leaders must catch your culture so they can carry it in every action and word they speak. Creating an atmosphere of faith is probably the one we see a lot of people struggle with. You can be a master at games and light and sound. But those things won't change a young person's life. Only an encounter with God will, and encountering God will happen when there is an atmosphere where the young person feels comfortable and safe, and like nobody else is watching. It's created by the tone we set from the stage and the words we speak. If we go after faith and presence and encounter, then young people will too.

Don't be afraid of ministry time. Don't tiptoe around the altar. As simple as this sounds, practice will make you more confident. Try different things from the stage. Prophecy! Bring certain groups of kids forward. Pray big prayers. Be sensitive to the Holy Spirit.

Setting an atmosphere is something you will constantly need to have your attention on. Don't force it with harsh words but encourage and reward moments when everyone gets it right. Done well, it's subtle and soft but one of the most powerful elements of your youth group.

ESSENTIAL 37

Earn parents' trust

We have two choices when it comes to parents. Either make them a friend or they could become an enemy. It's the difference between letting their kids come to youth or not.

Parents are entrusting you with the most precious thing they have in this life. They've raised these human beings from birth. The teenage years can be as big an adjustment for parents as for the kids. They are learning to give some rope, to let them go a little at a time and that can be pretty scary stuff. Parents would rather them be in a good youth ministry with you though, than any other place. You come from a strong place of trust. Don't mess it up. Don't lose that. Your job is to build credibility with them, which can be done easily.

Here's a few suggestions:

- ♥ Picks ups/drop offs

    You could be one of the first people they have allowed their kids to travel with in a car who is not a well-known friend or family member. That is a big deal for them and some basic manners will go a long way in establishing further trust:

- speak to the parent, not the child and ask if you may come and pick them up for youth/life group
- when you arrive, do not beep the horn. Go to the front door, knock and say hello to the parents
- let them know an estimated time when you will return their child and stick to it

♥ Phone calls

- when calling a young person, ask if you can quickly say hi to their parent. Believe us, they will be blown away
- ask the parent if there is anything you can do in anyway to help them with their child

♥ The drop off zone at Youth

If parents drop their kids to youth, they will form an opinion of you and your youth ministry from the carpark. Again there are some simple things you should do that will go a long way:

- have some mature leaders in the carpark to say a quick hello to parents as they drop their kids off
- remember parents' names
- if they get out of the car, shake their hand, or, if you know them, give them a hug
- make sure they can see sign in, which helps them ascertain that you are doing duty of care when it comes to looking after their child

♥ Visits

> When you take a young person on a visit, especially if they are very young, be sure to ask their parent for permission to do so first. Don't just make arrangements through the young person (unless you have established a good relationship over time). No parent ever begrudged a great role model wanting to spend time with their teenager.

From our parent heart to yours, and from decades of doing this for other people's kids, we are now in the reverse position – people doing it for us. We are so grateful. We are grateful to the group of girls who, the first time we dropped Georgia off at youth, gave me a hug like we were old friends. They had me at 'hello!'

We are beyond grateful to Celeste and Andy, who baptised Georgia and prayed over her with so much love, so much of God shone through from their hearts for her. The memory still makes us tear up. We are beyond grateful for other leaders, who have cared for Georgia through every single year of her teenage life, who have talked with her about bikinis and boys and God and taught her to love God's Word more than anything else. Thank you to Jake, who is in the middle of it all now with our boys. He shows them everyday what it is to be a man after God's own heart. He loves and leads them with strength. He is the kind of man we want our boys to be. Our breath is taken away by every single one of you. If a parent hasn't told you yet, they will tell you soon – *'We love you. You are changing our young person's life.'*

ESSENTIAL 38

Cars are more than wheels and metal

Sarah was a down to earth, no nonsense 19 year old leader who drove a nondescript station wagon. We have always told our leaders to come to youth with a car full and no one took this more seriously than Sarah. She and her car became a *Solid Rock* legend. In the days before such strict legal duties and rules, Sarah used to cram kids into her car. When she arrived at youth, the car doors and the boot burst open and the kids would spill out. I think the record was something like 10 kids. She squeezed them into every bit of space she could. Four in the back seat, a few in the wagon boot, two in the front passenger seat. Eventually we had to put a stop to it for safety reasons.

How we loved Sarah's enthusiasm though! We need more Sarah's. Our young people are desperate for them. Sarah understood the heart behind filling up your car. She understood that another kid in her car meant another kid in God's presence at youth. She knew it meant another kid who felt they belonged. It meant another conversation, another young life changed.

Our young people need our car. They need our petrol and the Macca's wrappers at their feet. They need our imperfect, squeaky, barely clean car. Your car is so much more than four wheels and hunk of metal. Your car is one of the most important things in a young person's life. My life was forever changed because my youth leader used to pick me up every week. She took me out of my dysfunctional, crazy home and made me feel loved and safe and like I had hope. Her car brought me to youth, the place I found family and home and my future. It hurtled me down the highway toward my destiny and I am so grateful to this day.

Later I got to do it myself for my young people. Some nights I would do two trips to connect group and home again, because I loved them so much and wanted them to experience God like I had. I would do anything for them.

It makes us sad when we see youth leaders driving into youth with empty cars. If every youth leader across the nation had a full car every Friday night, that would be quite a revival.

ESSENTIAL 39

Schedule a camp every 12 months

We were sitting on top of a windy hill with Byron Bay locals, eating chicken and pesto sandwiches and sipping a macadamia latte, on the way back from *Public Youth's* first ever camp. For us, it's around the 25th year of youth camps. We stopped counting maybe a decade ago. We were just discussing how funny it is, that after all these years we still love half pubescent, openly honest, unpredictable teenagers. They have our heart for all time. While others find themselves on professional speaking circuits, we find ourselves here, at old dodgy campsites like Camp Drewe. We wrestle with corded microphones and squealing speakers. We do it because we believe in camps and their power to transform young people, leaders and entire youth ministries.

Having camp once a year is an absolute must for any youth group, a bit like the obligatory dentist appointment only less painful – well most of the time anyway!

Camp takes effort, preparation and hours of unseen planning and preparatory work. Like lining up at the cheap shop to buy 10 bottles of dish-washing liquid and a dozen pool noodles. You pretend you don't know everyone is staring at you in the register line. It's early morning prayer meetings and cleaning rosters and tons of last minute phone calls to parents to get every last kid there. It's bake sales and car washes and basketball comps to fundraise and it's asking bosses for a few days off work. It's for a good cause.

Parents wave you off with stares of *'you better look after my kid'*. You finally land at camp, ready to swat anyone if they sing one more round of whatever bus song you've already heard 99 times. With no break to caffeinate a constant drip feed would be a great idea for camp! Can someone please invent one? Eventually you get everyone sorted in their luxurious accommodation before the first round of camp games begin.

We feel your pain. We've been there more times than we can remember. We've stayed up late, gotten up early and some nights got no sleep at all. We've done endless hours of 'pash patrol', keeping the boys in their quarters and girls in theirs. But over the space of two or three days, something happens that can take a year of Friday nights to evolve back at home. Maybe it's something to do with sharing three toilets for three days straight, or sitting around the camp-fire with only the stars for an audience or being forced to wash dishes together. But solid ten out of ten friendships are cemented in the memories only those in camp will share. Hearts are prized open and words spoken that just don't have time to come out on a Friday night. Young people bare their secrets to leaders who have been spending all their money on petrol for months to get them to this point. The point where they are ready to crack and spill open what they've been holding inside for a while. Their fears and their struggles.

But the best part, 'without a shadow of a doubt' is how worthwhile every bit of effort has been, when you see what happens in the meetings. It's holy and sacred and we will remember it for years to come, even the rest of our lives. It's that moment when the young person feels God for the first time. The moment when they realise God has been with them all along. The moment when they are first filled with the Holy Spirit or so filled with God himself, it's spilled out in tears. It's the moment they realise they are called and dreams are birthed, right there on the stained, worn, daggy campsite carpet.

For years we've used a certain pattern to guide our camp meetings. It goes like this:

Faith
Issues
Encounter
Testimonies

Faith

The first night sets the tone, builds faith, tells them what's to come. Set the standard you want to go for in praise, worship and teach them how to respond. Don't be too preachy or teachy on the first night. Create an atmosphere of great anticipation of what God is about to do in their lives.

Issues

First morning meeting, deal with issues, things of the heart. Have someone preach who is sensitive. It doesn't have to be a loud 'ra-ra' message. Give time for ministry and for young people to respond to God. Have leaders ready to pray, create space for them and God.

Encounter

Now you have prepared the soil and are ready to 'go for God'. For your night meeting, go for encounter. Find the key. Teach them to hunger for Him. Pray! Prophecy! Don't let any hang onto the edges, allowing them to spectate. Pull them all in.

Last night we were praying for kids to be filled with the Holy Spirit. Leaders were standing behind, a hand on their shoulder, whispering some prayers tentatively. So we taught them how to pray life-altering prayers over the young people. Stand in front of them, lean in and pray so they can hear you. Prophecy, speak life, be confident, have faith. Young people will take your lead. They will follow. You are their spiritual leader, not just their team leader. Believe God wants to do incredible things in the hearts of your young people and they will believe it too.

Testimonies

Finally, testimonies are a great way to end, usually on the last morning meeting. The Bible says we overcome by the blood of Jesus and the word of our testimony. It's powerful for young people to hear what God has done in another person's life. Young people will cheer their peers on as they get up to share. It helps cement what God has done. We can guarantee, you will be the one split open, undone. You will forget in a second any effort or pain it took to get to this moment.

Just a few hours ago, with quivering lips and water-filled eyes, our young people shared. *I tried to resist God but I couldn't. When you laid hands on me I felt the fire of God.* But the best testimony from Camp Drewe came in the form of a 13 year old, dark-haired boy. As Cameron was sitting down at the outdoor table after the meeting, this boy walked up and lunged into him with outstretched arms, his tiny body nestled into Cameron's shoulder for a full five seconds. The boy's tiny arms held on to Cameron, his only way to express how overwhelmed he was at all God had done for him. No words were required.

Thank you Camp Drewe for the moments now buried like secrets in your walls. We'll definitely see you again, same place, same time, next year. We can't wait.

ESSENTIAL 40

Create a Springbrook Mountain

We've often visit Aleesha and Tom's House. They live exactly one and a half hours from our place. We don't mind the drive. It's beautiful navigating through narrow winding roads where you feel miles away and the arms of a thousand trees bow over you in protection and you can't see the sky. The smell of rotting leaves and a freshly mown lawn fill the car. You feel refreshed as though you have flown to another place.

We pull up at their house, a simple drive of cobblestones hedged by wild growing lilly pillies. The door is already open, like the house itself is beckoning us in. Indi and Mila, five and three respectively, stand a short distance away in the yard. They are wearing each other's dresses, Indi with fairy wings on her back. Lying in front of them are two dolls covered only in leaves as blankets. Around their feet run three chickens, two black and one white. Behind them, in the corner of the garden, is a handmade, wooden cubby house, strung with lights that really work, a half dead lavender plant, an ironing board, a kitchen and a cash register. On the opposite side of the garden is a swing, tied on a tree branch by the longest ropes you ever saw. When you swing, it makes you feel light and airy and magical, like you never want to stop.

Our afternoon goes quickly, almost as though time doesn't exist in their part of the world. We walk to the nearby waterfalls, Mila on Tom's back and Indi on Cameron's. The little girls play with our big boys, tiptoeing through ankle deep water, toes squelching on algae covered rocks. After a while, with rosy cheeks and hemline soaked dresses, we pick our way back through the shortcut. We'd created new paths, pushing back vines and wading slowly through the creek, calling out encouragement to one another not to fall in. A neighbour they have never met comes out of his house to help us past a yard where two large, scary looking dogs sit on the roadside barking ferociously at us and we are all too petrified to pass by on our own.

Once back, Tom lights a fire and Aleesha grabs a bag of marshmallows. As the sun sets over the mountains, we roast marshmallows and talk about every-thing. As we drive away, saying a hundred goodbyes, thank you's and we love you guys, we almost don't want to go back to the city. They have discovered a little piece of paradise out there on Springbrook Mountain. But it isn't just the house or the place they live. It's something they carry inside of them and we want a little more of it.

It makes total sense now, why their girls are two of the most delightful little creatures we have ever met. We can hardly describe the calm, the innocence, the sense of a time gone by when we were with them. These girls are as sweet in their souls as their adorable little faces. They have a purity and gentleness that is hard to describe and it's no wonder. Indi and Mila are raised and held together with love and connection. They are being brought up bare-footed, wild in the forest and waterfalls of their backyards. They run and play and create. They imagine and role play, side by side where leaves become blankets and the outdoors is their kingdom. Very rarely do we see a phone or any kind of device in their hand. Even when we were at a coffee shop for a full hour and a half, they were content with their baby hot chocolates, a notepad and pen. Indie drew the salt and pepper shakers and the posy of flowers on the table. She wrote little notes for her mum. That's the other secret – contentment. They didn't winge and whine and ask for phones so they could watch Netflix or Peppa Pig.

We want to shout and clap and say well done to Tom and Aleesha. We need more of what you are giving your girls. Our generation of young people need it. We need it too.

One of the greatest challenges we all face is staying truly, deeply connected in a screen-driven world. Young people are so busy looking down they forget to look up. They are losing the art of connection and creativity and fun. They sit behind closed doors, 'talking' to each other on social media when what they really need is to be sitting around a fire, roasting marshmallows and talking about everything and nothing. In a world where too many are feeling more disconnected and lonely than ever before, Aleesha, Tom and their girls have each other. They come to us this way, because parents are mostly at a loss as well. The Tom's and Aleesha's of this world are rare. The ones that teach them from a young age how to have a conversation and look someone in the eye, in real time. Parents are trying their best but often feel defeated by the tidal wave of screen time addiction.

We can help. We can make a difference in the lives of these young people because we can create opportunities for connection and real time relationships. We can show them to value what happens when we put down our phone and look at someone directly. Truly look and really talk. Mental health issues have sky-rocketed in the past decade plus and although there's no direct proof, it suspiciously correlates with the time devices became a way of life, a rite of passage even for children. Self-esteem plummets as they compare and compete, scrolling through pictures of everyone else's 'perfect' lives.

Although social media is a wonderful way to communicate and another avenue to build community, it doesn't, shouldn't and can't replace face to face. Don't be afraid to set boundaries when it comes to screens in your youth ministry. We have been in youth groups where kids are constantly distracted on their phone. We can't stress enough the huge favour you are doing them, by setting a standard. Just like you don't allow them to chitter-chatter during the preaching time, a phone should be treated no differently. It can only distract them from engaging in the word and encountering God.

Our daughter went to an amazing youth ministry in her early teenage years. We are grateful for it to this day. We were absolutely thrilled when she went off each week with her Bible, (not a bible app!) a pen and notepad. That youth ministry created a culture of listening and leaning in and being present. Phones stayed in bags, muted or turned off.

It grew in her a love for God's Word and His presence. When we picked her up, we were always impressed to see everyone hanging around talking. It was a rare sight to see any young person on their phone. Their eyes were up. There was a buzz of chatter and activity and it spilled over into her everyday life. We'd find her, in her bedroom, pouring over her Bible, journal open beside her. She would monitor herself on social media, at times fasting from it of her own accord.

When we preach anywhere, we ask young people to put their phones away. Set the culture, tone and behaviour for your youth ministry. Set it by your own example. Set it by the words you speak, set it by the behaviours you demand. Go against the cultural norms and patterns and teach them to bring their Bibles and a notepad. Tell them that we don't have phones out during the service. Have leaders sitting with their young people, monitoring and encouraging. Be diligent. Be consistent. Before you know it, looking up instead of down will become the norm.

Young people crave a place to belong and people to care for them. Their well-being depends on being seen and accepted and loved deeply. We can give them that. Find your own Springbrook Mountain. Find a family willing to open their home. Find a back yard. Light a fire. Roast marshmallows. Sit around a table. Be family. Do family. Walk into the wild with them.

So thank you Tom and Aleesha, for reminding us not to lose our way, that there is still a better way if only we will work hard for it. Indi and Mila, may you always stay connected and free and as content as you were that day.

ESSENTIAL 41

Create sticky moments

There are moments in our lives that will transform us because they bring us closer to God or to others or both. We call these 'sticky moments' and with enough of these, the tale is a beautiful life full of meaning and purpose. Sticky moments are the light when the rest of life is the shade. They are a break from the in-between.

Sticky moments usually happen accidentally and yet we can plan for them. They sneak into our life and yet it's not wrong to strategise for them.

We can plan but ultimately it's up to God to breathe life into them. Sticky moments are memorable, like photos in an album. We look back and say 'remember when?'

One recent Friday night a gathering of our young adult community turned into one of these. We had been planning toward building some momentum amongst our young adults and we've tried a few different things. Picnic rugs and graze boards in the park. Burgers stuffed high with grilled chicken and pineapple and mayo after church. Small groups squeezed into lounges. These gatherings have all been good and wholesome and contributed in small ways to creating a belonging and a home. But something extra sweet and special happened that Friday night around a bonfire.

A group gathered, tired from a full week's work. They sat on logs for seats and roasted marshmallows held on sticks found on the ground. We weren't there but later in the night they sent us a video and photographs and we could see that magic had weaved its way into hearts, sticking them together in a most unlikely place – a backyard bonfire. 50 young adults sang into the night to guitar music while night time insects buzzed in the background. Their worship was pure and raw, as untouched as the earth under their feet. Flames from the fire threw light on their faces, eyes were closed, hearts abandoned to the moment. *'We live for you'...* they sang over and over. You could hear that it wasn't just words, it was their anthem. It was honest and they meant it.

After worship they shared, in twos and threes. They opened up, telling their stories of how they came to be there, what they thought they needed, and what made them most afraid. Looking through the photos, we could see the difference between the ones taken at the beginning of the night and the ones taken nearer the end. Their arms were no longer around one another, posing for a polite photo, they were entangled and held on tightly to each other, unguarded.

Earlier there were spaces between them, now there were none. They had been filled by love and acceptance. Something special that had happened as the fire burned. Something truly special had happened in our young adult community, something we'd been praying for and wanting for a long time. In one night, a planned but unplanned sticky moment turned them from acquaintances into friends, confidants not just talkers. It had fast-tracked friendships. It did in one night what can take months or even years to develop.

Look out for the sticky moments with your teams and with your young people. They can happen at an altar, around a prophecy, or in worship. They can happen while sharing at a discipleship or connect group. It could be a moment at a camp or around a fire, from a conversation in the car or while eating ice-cream from a cup. It can happen while you serve together, pray together or eat together.

You can feel it, when you've had one of these moments. It's like something sacred has taken place and one can only whisper about it. Plan for them but know that that cannot be forced. They must happen with a rhythm and timing all of their own. But when they do, mark them well for you will look back one day and fondly say – *'remember when!'*

ESSENTIAL 42

Behaviour management is crucial in youth ministry

Every year we held our camp at Zintari, Normanville, South Australia. It was the only campsite in the State large enough to hold us all. Our youth ministry was growing rapidly and we always put a huge focus on camp, doing everything we could to get every single young person there. Our camps had a long history of seeing young people encounter God in powerful ways, so for us they were a big focus.

Our camps were always held in the dead of winter. Knowing how bitterly cold Adelaide winters are, I have no idea what we were thinking. But the leaders and young people didn't seem to mind. In the mornings there was a scurry to the showers, everyone wrapped in sleeping bags and blankets as they darted over, hoping to be the beneficiary of the hottest water possible. The day began with steaming cups of hot chocolate in the dining hall, hoping that hot liquid would reach our frozen toes.

But aside from the meetings, our favourite part was the bonfire at night. It was the only time we were truly warm, hot even, as we sat around far into the night roasting marshmallows and talking. The bitter cold air and dark night sky dotted with sparkling stars and the comfort of the crackling fire always weaved its magic into our hearts, causing us to split open and share our deepest thoughts in ways that never seemed to happen in the light of day. Those nightly bonfires became a tradition.

One night some of the students escaped the meeting early to start the bonfire themselves. By the time we arrived, we were duly impressed with their efforts. *Where did you get all the wood,* we asked. *Oh, we just pulled apart the old wagon that had been sitting over there.* Their white teeth shone in the dark night, pleased with their efforts. Our eyes wandered over to the space where the old wagon had been sitting. It had been there every year that we had been having camp and suddenly our hearts sank. That old wagon, that had taken only minutes to tear apart with their bare hands, was a one hundred year old antique, the pride of the camp owners. That little piece of Zintari history was now ablaze in front of us, disappearing into ash and dust. Needless to say, we were banned from ever returning to that campsite again!

What we have to discern about behaviour and discipline when it comes to teenagers, is the motive. The motive should therefore determine our approach and strategy. Some behaviour is purely the result of their age. It's a young person being a young person. It's innocent, unintentional mistakes made by brains that haven't fully developed yet. The wagon was one of those moments. If they had realised the wagon was a one hundred year old piece of history that really belonged in a museum, there was no way they would have touched it. When misbehaviour is unintentional, there is still a consequence, but you don't have to correct or discipline their moral heart. You can talk them through it, have them admit their error and do what they can to repair the damage. In this case, there was nothing much they could do except give their sincerest apologies to the owner.

However the kind of behaviour that does need to be addressed is the kind that is intentional and comes from a rebellious heart and a wilful mind. We need to have higher expectations of young people's behaviour. Some leaders are unwilling to set strong boundaries, using the excuse that they are at youth and not in school. But we have found that high expectations coupled with strong boundaries and clear consequences actually make for a much better youth ministry. Young people will rise to the levels that you set. They feel safe when they know what the rules and expectations are.

Youth is actually no different from a classroom. We should expect respectful, well-mannered young people. Young people highly respect a youth leader whose word is their word and who demands respect and good standards of behaviour. Like a bloodhound, they will smell you a mile off if you doubt your own authority and are too scared to discipline. You will not lose young people from your youth ministry for disciplining consistently when required. In fact, you will gain them. Parents will not send their teenagers to a youth group where poor behaviour goes unchecked and dominates the culture.

One youth ministry we visited had students from a particular school running rings around the youth leaders. They walked in and out of meetings, talked back to leaders, were on their phone most of the time and were known to be rough and disrespectful. This wasn't the only problem with this youth group. General behaviour management was poor and we said to each other as we drove home that it was only a matter of time before there was an accident or a fight. Unfortunately, we were right. A few months later, a young person had a nasty bone break during a game. We know accidents happen but the lack of boundaries and discipline certainly contributed to the way that particular incident unfolded. We had spoken to a number of parents from that church who said they didn't send their kids to the youth ministry because of the lack of behaviour management.

We have always and continue to set high standards of behaviour in our youth ministry. When young people know that you love them and believe in them, they respond beautifully to boundaries. The keys are to know what your standards are and to be consistent, demanding nothing less and to have clear consequences for bad behaviour.

Here's a few things we have insisted on over years:

Everyone stands up during worship.

It is possible to make this happen because we always explain the why behind our what. We tell them that by standing, we are showing respect for God and for our friend next to us, who wants to engage in worship. We scattered leaders amongst them, who would remind anyone who decided their 'legs were too tired'. We set the tone that we are family and family do things together, including worship.

No toilet trips during the meeting.

We are not dealing with two year olds who can't hold their bladder. They don't go to the toilet every two seconds at school, so neither should they in youth. We give them time at the start and the end. If they are busting, we will allow them to go one at a time – which usually takes the fun out of the real reason behind the toilet trip. With no friend to waste time with, a toilet trip alone becomes boring and suddenly they don't need to go anymore.

Nobody walks out of the meeting.

Apart from the fact we have a duty of care, there is no need to wander out of the meeting. We always chose very specific leaders to be on the doors – the bouncer looking type who wouldn't be talked around by anyone but would send them back to their seat with no arguments.

Phones away during the meeting.

This is a hard one and something that has changed rapidly, especially since our young pastoring days in Adelaide. But even now when we preach somewhere, we set the expectation from the stage by telling them we want their phones put away for the next few minutes. Give them a reason such as, 'I'll only speak for a short time and I don't want you to miss out'. Let them know the consequences in a light-hearted manner, such as, 'If I see a phone I will come and get it', then lighten it up with a joke. You can believe us when we say, we have gotten off the stage and taken a phone or two. You can't stop everyone from looking at their phone, but at least this way it stops the group texting and people sitting next to one another laughing and distracting everyone around them because of whatever is on their screen. If we ran a youth ministry every week, we would be going for a 'phones away' rule.

You don't talk while the person on the stage is talking.

This is teaching good, reliable, life-skill kind of manners. If we're talking we don't expect students to talk over us. Again, it will only take a few reminders from the stage to set this culture.

Whatever culture you go for is what you will get. What you allow will continue. Rather than tell them what you don't want, keep reinforcing what you do want and who you are as a youth ministry. It's powerful to set your culture by the things you consistently speak of. For example, at our youth, we all bring our Bibles and take notes; at our youth, we stand up and show respect to God and worship together.

Having clear consequences in mind for those who still won't fall in line is also important. You only have to discipline them once or twice for them to know that you mean what you say and you will follow through with consequences. Everyone around them will get the message too. It makes everyone feel safe, including parents who are trusting you with their young person.

We had a two strike policy. They received two warnings and if you don't change your behaviour, you're banned for a week. When you return and if you continue to misbehave, you will lose the privilege of coming to youth for a term. During that time, we'd visit them and continue to stay connected. For the most part, these young people not only came back but went on to become core youth, even leaders.

At first our leadership team was suspicious of this tough love. But when they saw the results in the changed culture of our youth ministry and in the lives of our young people, they became the biggest advocates of our behaviour management approach. At the end of the day, we knew we were not curbing behaviours but disciplining hearts. We had a long term approach, not a knee jerk reaction out of frustration or anger. It was no wonder our youth ministry was growing quicker than we could keep up, because we built so much trust and respect from parents at our church, they were almost pushing their young people out the car and into our care.

ESSENTIAL 43

Any time is the best time for salvation invitations

John was a rough around the edges kid in our youth group who mostly came either because his mum made him or there was a girl there he liked. We took him whichever way he came. He might have been physically present but his heart was far removed and guarded from us and from God.

He was also the kid that took his parents' car for a joy ride in our church carpark on a Sunday evening and crashed it.

Everyone was worried about John but we have a fondness for these young people who are messy and don't want to stay between the lines. Most of them have a great leadership calling on their lives.

One Friday night we were finishing up our series on dating. At the end, we did what we always do – an opportunity for young people to respond to a salvation invitation. It didn't matter what we were doing at youth, we had been taught to end on that. Because what if that meeting was the only time a young person was at a place where they would get to hear the message of Jesus? The Holy Spirit can and is prompting young hearts. He doesn't rely on us to have preached a brilliant soul-saving message or be playing tender, moving music or have the lights dimmed. Atmosphere is important but God does not rely on us for these things. He has already been working on and poking at their hearts, preparing and softening them.

So that Friday night we gave an opportunity for a salvation response right after talking about dating and relationships. We'll never forget that night. Even before we had finished speaking, John's head emerged from the crowd as he almost ran to the altar. With tears in his eyes, he gave his life back to God again. He left his independent wilfulness at the altar and walked back a changed boy. We were all shocked because we couldn't fathom what he had heard in our chat about dating that prompted him to run back to God that day. But God doesn't need our fancy words when He is already palm deep in a heart.

Never discount an opportunity for God to move on a young person. Use every opportunity to offer them salvation. We don't remember any youth or church meeting in Adelaide when this didn't happen. It's no coincidence that our church was one of the greatest soul winning churches we have ever seen to this day.

PART 4
TRANSFORMING YOUTH

ESSENTIAL 44

True care transforms young people

This part of the book should be far longer than it is! There are so many things to be said about how to help our young people. Maybe we will write a whole book on this.

For now, we have picked some of our top essentials.

In reality and in our travels, most youth groups are not doing pastoral care as effectively as it can be done. Pastoral Care conjures up different thoughts and ideas.

This is where leaders could switch off because they think 'been there, done that'.

We even tried to think of a more alluring name than 'pastoral care' but we kept coming back to it every time. Most youth leaders have never been shown how to care fully, for young people but when you do, it changes entire youth ministries and lives.

First, let's look at what pastoral care isn't.
It's NOT

- ♥ a text message
- ♥ a social media dm
- ♥ a conversation at church on a Sunday morning
- ♥ a chat on the bleachers on a Friday night
- ♥ counting how many people you had at connect group and reporting that to your leader
- ♥ a car trip
- ♥ haphazard care by whichever leader wants to connect with whatever young person
- ♥ a quick chat at connect group

As good as some of these are, they alone do not form a good enough basis for real, authentic, lasting care. Each of the above are things we should be doing with our young people, but effective pastoral care is much more than this. It must be intentional, planned for and carefully implemented and monitored.

So let's look at what pastoral care is.

We can't go past good systems for effective pastoral care. You absolutely cannot do effective pastoral care without a system that the entire youth team uses weekly. The system isn't the care but it drives the care. It means the entire team is clear on exactly who is caring for whom and when and how that is happening. Systems help to measure how well your pastoral care is being done.

When our son played football, the players didn't all run on the field and play wherever they wanted. There was a plan and they couldn't expect to win without one. In fact winning depended on it. The field was divided into three and every man had his position and specific places he could and couldn't go. Players mostly stayed in the same position for the whole season. The rules weren't to restrict, they were for success.

Pastoral care in a youth ministry is no different. You want to win, so you have to plan for it. There needs to be rules, boundaries, positions and a clear plan. Here are our top tips for effective pastoral care.

- ❤ Make sure every young person who comes to your youth and church is on your database. Sounds obvious, but how accurate is your database?
- ❤ Allocate every single young person on your database immediately into a connect group, including and especially new people and new Christians.
- ❤ Decide how your connect groups are sorted

    - Year levels
    - Gender
    - Suburbs

We arrange ours according to suburbs to make them easy for parents to drive to. We mix boys and girls together as well as year levels for several reasons. One is that boys and girls like to be in each other's company, which makes them want to be at connect even more. Another is that we like to emulate real life. It's only school that separates young people into age groups but for the rest of their lives they will be mixing with all ages. There's no better way than doing it in the presence of youth leaders, who can help them wade through the turbulent and at times tricky waters of teenage friendships.

♥ Allocate a leader and an assistant leader to be responsible for each group and ideally have them stay in that group for at least a year, preferably more. It's quite common in youth ministry for students to have the same leader throughout their high school years. Ensure these leaders are very clear on their role, especially pastorally, as connect group leaders.

♥ Create a spreadsheet (or something similar) with a list of names for each connect group. These lists should include:
- name and details
- attendance to youth/connect/church
- dates they been contacted by phone AND visited
- extra notes

Why do we do this? Because writing it down makes it very clear who has been cared for and who has been missed. If you have no specific plan your pastoral care will be chaotic, hit and miss, sporadic.

It shows you who has not come for a while so you can make a call or pop by to see if the family is ok. It also ensures pastoral care is spread evenly and you don't have one youth who has been visited five times by three different leaders and another not at all.

♥ The youth pastor should check every connect group spreadsheet every week

It's healthy for each connect leader to know they are accountable to the youth pastor. Not only did we check every connect group spreadsheet weekly, but every leader texted basic details to us after each connect was finished.

♥ Dedicate 10-15 mins discipleship to each pastoral care visit.

This way all the leaders know how valued care is within the youth ministry. There's nothing like asking a question about any young person on a list to keep leaders accountable.

♥ New Christians and New People should be a top priority

How well are these young people being looked after in your youth ministry?

Here are a few ideas on how this can be done:

- allocate one person to follow up the care of all new people and new Christians
- contact new people/new Christians by the following Tuesday after youth
- introduce them personally to their connect leaders
- follow up for a month or more to ensure they are integrated and connected into their connect group
- provide a new Christian program, like Alpha, to help them learn the basics of their faith

♥ Phone calls are extremely effective

Conversation in real time can make them feel valued, important and loved. The human voice will never be replaced by a text. (more on this the next Essential)

Recording who you call, helps you to look after everybody and not just a random few.

♥ Visits are a must

This is one of the most important aspects of pastoral care. Visiting communicates care and changes the lives of young people more than anything else.

- Schedule them
Plan for them. We had goals for our team, like trying to visit two students a week. Whatever fits your schedule.

Usually our connect groups had about 30 young people, so our goal was that every student in our youth ministry would get at least one visit a term.

- Build relationship with the parents
Ask the parents if you can take their young person out. Get permission. Build relationship with the parents. They'll be so grateful to you.

- Record the visit
Again this needs to be confidential but is a way to communicate how the students are travelling to the youth pastor. It's also for your own record to ensure everyone is being cared for.

- Have conversations that count
There are no rules or guidelines for this except to say the most effective leaders are by far the ones who get elbow deep into the lives of their students.

It's conversations over coffee and turning up for moments, like a sports game or gradation.

It's asking the soul searching questions and praying with them. Then remembering what they said for the next time you're together and asking how they are going with that.

It's praying in the car before you visit them, asking God for your conversation to lead to places in their heart that He only would know about.

Visits are about getting into their world and learning what they love, what bothers them, where they've been and what makes them tick.

It's speaking encouragement and words that breathe life, filling them up for those moments when the world comes in full force to deplete them.

It's knowing which weekend they are with their mum and when they are staying at Dad's, or remembering their birthday and the anniversary of a loved one's death. Knowing who they want to be when they leave school and cheering them on as they work toward that.

It's swimming at the beach and sitting in silence until the sun goes to sleep and trying on ridiculous outfits at op shops that make you laugh until your insides ache.

This is what turns acquaintances into friends and friends into family. This is how you become their people. This is what happens when pastoral care works the way it should – you become their people.

We've just watched our daughter walk out the gates of high school for the very last time. While her high school friends were walking slowly, almost sadly, making plans to catch up in a few days or next week, her steps were quick and fast. 'I'm not sad,' she said. 'I'm so happy.' We knew why. It was because she has her people. She's going to have them the rest of her life, like we have. They weren't found within the walls of her classroom or inside the school gates.

That didn't happen because they texted her or had a ten minute chat after youth. It happened in the in between. During the pauses and commas of life nestled between the big moments. The word 'visit' doesn't do it justice really. More like a pilgrimage, a sojourn, a journey together. That's where a leader becomes your kinfolk and the youth group your people.

ESSENTIAL 45

Phone calls are a game changer

I t's easy to text, or leave a message on social media, or ask how someone is doing on messenger. It's become an acceptable thing to do.

Yesterday, during one of our Online Academy Info sessions, one of our students said, 'You guys changed my life and leadership and you wouldn't even know it. You taught me to pick up the phone.'

In a world of ease and convenience, we mustn't forget the power of some 'old school' connection. Popping by on social media is fabulous but it won't replace the connections built by real time conversation.

When we first suggest to *Academy* students that they pick up the phone and talk to their young people, they look absolutely horrified. Usually it's because they have some unexplained fear of actually calling somebody. We have become the master of hiding behind keypads. It requires less of us. Less time, less effort, less vulnerability. They wonder at us. What would we say? Why are we calling? It's odd and awkward to actually talk to somebody.

So we give them all the reasons why they should. We tell them how this creates a deeper connection than a text. For a human to hear the voice of another human, it comforts beyond what a text message and an emoji can do. It forces you to go deeper, ask questions. Despite how silent a young person can be at the other end, it makes them feel connected, cared for and deeply loved. It is only awkward if we make it awkward. Learn to break through those moments. Reignite the art of conversation. Have a list of questions you can ask and if all else fails, just talk anyway.

There have been countless studies about all the hormones and nerves that fire in our brains when we hear the voice of someone we care about.

At first the *Academy* students make calls because we set it as a task. Weeks turned to months and without exception, those who persist come back wide-eyed and smiling hard. It literally changes the way they lead. It forges deep connections quickly and they see their connect groups grow. Phone calls are actually a game-changer. We used to drive twenty minutes to the church every Tuesday before connect group and call our entire group, mostly because our parents didn't like or want to pay for all the calls on their next phone bill. We sat in offices, every phone taken. Each list usually had around 20-30 young people, so that's a lot of talking. It's a lot of connecting, and caring.

Texts and social media are great for quick reminders, light connection and passing on information, but young people will tell you they aren't as connected to leaders who only use these means of communication. Leaders who take time and effort to connect in real time are the ones who make the greatest impact. We can tell you but why don't you try it for yourself? Pick up the phone, make a few calls and see the difference.

ESSENTIAL 46

Talk about dumb stuff and God stuff

As we shared in essential 44 on pastoral care, we can't build deep and meaningful connections with our young people only on the bleachers on a Sunday morning, or by a quick chat at youth on a Friday night. They need more from us.

Many of our young people are living in homes where they don't feel safe or heard or nurtured. Even those who do are wading the tumultuous waters of hormones and friendship dramas and stuff that matters so much when you are 13 and 14 years of age.

Youth leaders are some of the most powerful people in the lives of our youth. Many are forming shallow connections that can happen when they spend so much time only on screens. In fact, on average, teenagers check their phones 80 times a day. Although the data is just beginning to emerge, there seems to be a growing connection between the ratio of screen time and a young person's happiness. The more screen time in the earlier, developing years of a teenager, the higher their chances of feeling a deep sense of unhappiness. Enter you. You are a powerful force in that young person's life.

Spending time, taking them out, driving them around, having conversations, it's what is needed to see lives changing. We are huge advocates of visiting young people, like we said in the previous chapter. We keep our leaders accountable because we've seen its impact for decades now. When you take them out, let your conversations have a balance between talking about 'dumb stuff' and God stuff.

Conversations about 'dumb stuff' are necessary to building bonds between you. It's the silly stuff, the random stuff, the 'Whatever is on Your Mind Right Now' stuff. There is actually nothing dumb about it really. This generation doesn't want you to be their best friend but they do want to know that you care about the things they care about. Talking randomly is a powerful way to silently communicate that you love them. They need the petrol in your car and the drive through ice-creams. They need those moments when you belly laugh over the YouTube videos. They feel like the most important person in the world when you rock up to their school play or graduation and embarrass them with your cheers and whistles.

A few years ago now our youngest, Ashton, graduated year 6. We invited Joey to come, a young man that Ash looks up to. We were an unsightly bunch walking into the school hall that day, Cameron and I with Joey alongside, pierced, tattooed and long-haired, Ashton's friends stood and watched with mouths open. Ashton was so proud as he walked across the stage and delivered his School Captain's speech and the whole hall could hear our claps and cheers. At the end of the night, we took a photo that has become a favourite to this day because it says what can't be captured in words. Joey lifted Ashton up and there he sat on his shoulder, his favourite person, holding tight and smiling wide.

What a prophetic picture for a generation. They need our shoulders. They need us to believe in them, love them and lift them up. How proud Ashton was to have Joey there that day. Why did Ashton pick him? They talk about dumb stuff a lot of the time. About boxing and writing; the things Ashton loves. Because they talk about dumb stuff, he listens when Joey talks about God stuff too. His words carry weight and meaning, impressing on his heart, branding him as belonging to God.

Whenever you catch up with young people, go with two intentions. Dumb stuff and God stuff. Pray in the car on the way for God to open your eyes, help you see what this young person needs. Establish relationship and build a foundation by talking everyday stuff and then dive deep, like a scuba diver, looking for pearls at the bottom of the ocean. Dig for the gold, for the precious and rare parts of them. Gently put your hands into their chest to see where the painful parts are. Speak healing words over them, like how much God loves them and cares for them and has incredible plans for them. This is how we will change a generation, one visit at a time.

ESSENTIAL 47

May your words build their future

Caring for young people involves more than sitting down and talking about their problems. There is certainly space for you to be the one to reach inside and help them untie the knots, but don't over-talk their problems. Remember we spoke about how Russell has prophetic eyes, like he and God seemed to share the same breath. It's because Russell always seemed to know and understand the purpose God had put deep on the inside of us. He would call it out with words of hope. Instead of going over and over the negatives, he spoke over and over in the positives. Russell never told us what we couldn't do. He'd always tell us what we could do.

We are not here to raise a nice generation, one who will do lovely, safe things. We are here to raise a God generation, who know deep down in their gut that they have been put on this earth to live out a Call, who will wake up in the morning with vision and purpose, full of life and grit and determination. A generation who will fight to do what God has put inside of them, who are strong on the inside, resilient and risk-takers. We can help build resilience by speaking hope and telling them all of the wild, crazy, off the path things they can achieve. In a time in history where young people are wrapped in cotton wool for safety, duty of care and procedures, we are at risk of making them afraid to step out and become wild risk-takers for the purposes of God.

When I first met Sam and Russell, I was a very shy girl from a broken home. I emerged from a middle class suburb in Adelaide, rejected and insecure. Inside I loved God deeply. My lips uttered barely a word but I was filled with adventure and purpose. I had no idea what this would look like. All I knew was that I loved God and wanted to do something to help people to honour Him.

My mum moved us to Paradise Church the month after she married my step-dad because there was a youth group with a great reputation there. I entered a building that day and collided with my destiny. I could feel it.

God was in and around me. He consumed all of me and Russell and Sam could see it too. They told me marvellous things, like God had called me to preach, that He'd called me to the Nation. They prophesied that my life would make an incredible difference and that if you could graph my life, it would just keep going up and up. People would wonder at what God was doing in and through me.

Their words did something inside of me. They made me believe that crazy dreams could come true and even broken girls with wounded hearts could be used by God. Their words built me up to accept my future. It was like a piece of art being created in front of my eyes. The pieces turned this way and that, like a puzzle, creating an entirely new and incredible future for me. But it wasn't to be for a year or two. They spoke words like this for over 10 years, 15 years. Their words mixed with the breath of God carried me to the life I now live. They created a future I never imagined could be mine.

Decades later, when Georgia was old enough to go to youth, we chose a youth ministry that would do the same for her. We didn't want her to grow up to do a nice job and have a lovely Instagram account. We wanted leaders for her who would prophetically see into her soul and call out her God potential. Leaders who could speak out the things that were to be her destiny. Leaders who would tell her she was put on this earth to deliver the sweet sounds of God to the next generation. It was in that youth group we discovered she could sing – more than sing, that she was a worshipper. When she opened her mouth the soothing presence of the Holy Spirit would fill a room. It was there that God began to matter to her, so much that she began to yearn for a life centred around Him.

The creative power of a word spoken at the right time over a long period of time, is the stuff that miracles are made of. Your words mixed with God's words, can be a catalyst to changing a life. We have witnessed it over and over again. May your mouth hold miracles today and always.

ESSENTIAL 48

Turn self-harm into self-care

They want us to know, but they don't want to tell us. So they communicate by cutting, marking, burning, harming themselves. Some will cover it, wearing long sleeves even in hot weather. Others will not mind you seeing. It's confronting to see scars, fresh or old, on the inside of arms and thighs. It's hard to know what to do. Do we ignore it? Do we ask? We are not psychologists or counsellors, but we care for these young people and our hearts bleed invisibly while their cuts bleed for real. This is a massive topic to tackle but we suggest you look further into it and always seek expert help. Below we've outlined some things to get you started, because the reality is, you will come across young people who struggle with self-harm.

Self-harm is a cry for help and a cry of pain. It's just another way of saying I'm broken and I don't know how to fix it. Other young people will starve themselves or binge eat. They drink and take drugs. They Netflix binge or numb themselves by gaming. They are different but the same – *when my body can focus on another kind of pain, I don't have to think about the real source of my pain.*

When a young person cuts themselves, their body releases endorphins.

Stress + cutting = relief

The high of cutting is quickly followed by a low and both are addictive. It's more about a way of thinking than a behaviour. They have built a pathway in their brain that says *when I'm stressed if I cut, I experience relief.*

Of course other carers should be involved in helping these young people heal, but we want to put a tool in your hands too because often these young people will open up to a youth leader quicker than to any other authority figure in their lives.

Self harm is a symptom of something that is going on deep inside of them. It's making visible the pain that is kicking around silently in them. The pain is like a monster they can feel, under their skin and in their head. When cutting gives relief the first time, the second time and the third, then the neural pathways become deep and entrenched and they see it as their only way out, their only way to relief. Pathways are built quickly, reinforced by the sensory component.

But the relief that comes from harming is short lived and creates more problems than it solves. Often they feel more shame and guilt afterwards plus it prevents them from learning more effective strategies for feeling better.

A youth pastor/leader can be a huge support for a young person who engages in self harm. One of the most effective things you can do is to help them take action to move them toward building new pathways in their brain. You can be there for them and help them move over that peak and curb the urge. The key is self-care.

Stress + self care = relief

We can help young people by showing them ways to self-care. First, we do these things with them, so they will learn to do them when they are on their own. The goal is to move them toward the ability to do these things for themselves. Then they learn to self-regulate their emotions and to soothe and calm themselves.

There are many ways we can teach our young people to self-care. It's a great idea to build these ideas around the young person's interest. Here are some examples:

- go for a run with them
- kick the football together
- walk and talk
- shop and talk
- take them to a café and have coffee
- watch funny YouTube videos together

If you can't physically get to where they are, then try these:

- have a breathing app set up on their phone so they can do breathing exercises
- send them funny videos
- suggest they move rooms and change their environment
- read the Bible and do a devotion
- suggest that they go and shoot a few hoops
- watch their favourite light-hearted Netflix show
- talk to them over the phone
- pray for them over the phone

If you can teach them to do these things, it will help them get over the hump, around the mountain and the urge that will be the strongest around the first hour. Every time they self-care instead of self-harm, new neural pathways will be built in their brain. The self-care behaviours replace self-cutting behaviour. It teaches them practical things they can do when you might not be around. You are giving them the tools to delay self-harm and distract themselves until they can make the decision not to go ahead with it.

When you talk with them, use soothing language. Stay soft, calm and close, not fuelling what they're already feeling with a strong emotion. Physical touch, like a gentle arm around them, is another powerful way to help move them gently over that peak.

Then there's hope – the beautiful, powerful anchor of hope. Your presence gives arms and legs, breath and voice to whatever seems to elude them. You can gently bring it back to them and tell them it's going to be okay. Don't underestimate the power of you in their lives. You represent the thousand beautiful things waiting for them. You are the sunshine when all they feel is rain. You are their reminder that it's okay to be broken, because that's the way the light gets in.

If you would like to learn more about this topic, we highly recommend Michelle Mitchell's book, *Self-Harm: Why Teens Do It and What Parents Can Do To Help.*

ESSENTIAL 49

Be family to kids living out of a suitcase

L iving out of a suitcase is usually something to be celebrated, because it means you're on holiday or sleeping at your best friend's house or at the very least away from the normal rhythms and movements of everyday life. It means a welcome interlude, a change to the beat of the music of a normal day. It means beaches and late night swims in pools, tacos or pizza on a hill somewhere far away from home.

For at least a third, sometimes more of young people you might bump into, a suitcase means something completely different. It means they move between two addresses, two homes, two families. It means they own two sets of clothes in two different wardrobes and eat at two different dining tables. It means two sets of neighbourhood friends, two bedrooms, two couches. But for at least a third of young people, living in a broken home is normal. Normal is the lie we have come to believe, that because something is common, it must be normal. However, living in a broken home, families splitting in two and playing out in separate homes is not normal. Just ask anyone for whom this is reality.

Imagine a number of widowed families living in the same street together. Would we say the pain is any less for each family, for each child left without a father or mother, just because it is common in that street? Pain experienced en masse, doesn't make the pain normal and it certainly doesn't make it any less painful for each individual experiencing its sting.

Since we've swallowed the lie, along with most other people, about this new normal way of living, we have forgotten to tend to young people trapped in these circumstances in the special ways they need. Most places we go and speak, we are compelled to call these youth out and lay hands on them and speak to their broken souls. Every time as they come toward us, we see them bleeding out even before our arms can reach them. There will usually be tears trickling down faces, or heaving sobs that come from somewhere deep down, a place they might not have known existed. It's a relief when someone comes along and tells them we see and more importantly, that God sees.

We did this at the *Youth Alive Conference* in South Australia a few years ago. As we finished up and moved to the side of stage, the director, Sam Long was there, wiping the tears from his face with the back of his hand. *I didn't know there were so many*, he whispered. *There's just so many.*

I get it because I am one of them. I lived in two houses, my life stretching across Adelaide with Mum and holidays in Sydney with Dad. I knew that we weren't made to have two families, but that the pain of never fully belonging in either home can cut your soul so deeply you want to call SOS. You're not even sure if anyone would come to the rescue if you did. I understand two birthdays and Christmas in two places. Two people turning up for sporting events or a graduation, on opposite sides of the field, or perhaps no one turning up at all.

As these young lives stand before us at altars, their vulnerable eyes piercing ours, they almost look relieved that they aren't going crazy and someone has acknowledged their suspicions, that this has affected them in a profound way. There's a certain comradery amongst those of us from broken homes. We don't even have to explain to one another the cast of characters that come and go in our lives – step-mum, step-dad, boyfriends, girlfriends, step-grandparents, half-siblings, step-siblings. It's almost a comical rivalry between us of who has the longest list. We laugh at our crazy, shared problems, like how we get in trouble because we left our homework at dad's but tonight we're sleeping at mum's and how we can't remember which family's turn it is to spend Christmas with this year.

We can't begin to tell you what this does to us, deep down where it's dark and damp and nobody else can see unless they dig.

We need you, youth pastor, youth leader, because the one thing we have never had is a truly safe place to belong. For the most part, we know our mum and dad and families love us. But they didn't love us enough to stay together. They didn't love us enough to work it out, to plough on and fix what they broke. So this is where you come in. What we want, more than anything, is a place to belong.

In studies done on people from broken homes, it has been discovered that those who fare the best, in the long run, are those who find a place to belong, such as a youth group.

Some of the most important work done amongst young people is getting to know their story. Getting amongst it. As leaders, we expect them to come to us – be present at youth and connect group. But do we know who brings them? Or that they can't get there when they stay at dad's? Do you try to see what Christmas looks like for them this year, or where they will spend their holidays?

One of the most profound things we can do is to ask questions. Dig into the tangled mess of their lives. Be family to them because if family is measured by the amount of love one gives, many of us would qualify.

My pastors, Russell and Sam, were my second Mum and Dad. I hung at their house and one of the best gifts they gave me was allowing me to watch and see how family unfolded for them. I didn't watch from the sidelines, like part of an audience in the bleachers. They pulled me in and let me be one of them. I sat at their table and ate creamy pasta and crusty bread. Sam showed me how to cook. We'd sit curled up on the lounge with steaming cups of coffee. I found healing, not just at the altar, but in the home of good, godly people whom I adored. I drove in the car with them, buckled up in the backseat like their child. I don't know if they ever fully comprehended what they did for me. But by being part of a stable family, I began to heal.

They spoke promises over me, like *you're going to have a beautiful family of your own one day.* When I couldn't muster enough courage to hold on to a dream as breathtaking as that, they would hold it for me, until it actually came true.

The Bible says that God sets the lonely in families. It's the sweetest promise to every young person living in a broken home right now. We are God's living promise to these young people. Be their family. Remind them that their past will not define their future. Hold the dream for them, for those too scared to believe on their own, that they will belong to someone someday, in the most stunning and tender of ways.

Turn up, in the most ordinary and hum drum moments that when gathered together, look like life. Like coffee after school or cheering them on from the side-lines at their netball or football, with streamers and yelling and anything that will cause embarrassment, because that is what real family do. Check in on where they will spend Christmas Day and if they need you to help them shop for gifts. Let the healing power of belonging and love weave its magic deep into the dark places of their soul, giving them hope as an anchor to grasp.

Maybe one day, when we call out these young people to the altar, hardly anyone will come. Their suitcases will be packed away, left to collect dust on top of a wardrobe somewhere and we will be delighted because together, we helped love a generation to heal and saw the miracle of God's restoring power.

ESSENTIAL 50

Youth group is crucial for the well-being of Gen Z

As older role models and mentors, we know how to stop, look up and look around. In a world where our young people live most of their lives with their eyes down, our example is critical to them.

Most young people will attribute today's growing mental health crisis to screens and technology. Yet they have become such an integral part of our day to day lives that nobody wants to entertain the thought of giving them up. Although these devices haven't been in our world long enough for firm data to prove it beyond a shadow of doubt, what we are seeing is a correlation between technology and happiness. As levels of screen time have increased, levels of personal happiness are seen to have decreased. Despite a lack of critical data at the moment, we can certainly draw some conclusions that all this screen time and technology is not contributing to better health and well-being, in the same way that we know real time connections and relationships do.

More than ever before, this generation is pressured to present a picture perfect life where they have become a personal brand that they must continuously cultivate. It is exhausting. But how many youth pastors and leaders are doing exactly the same thing? We are no longer a pastor called into ministry by God. We have become a brand that must be constantly evolving and promoted. Social media is a wonderful thing, a place to be creative and tell our story. But not if it is in exchange for our true, vulnerable selves and our well-being.

Our youth groups will always be crucial in providing face to face connections that screens cannot give. It's the depth of these connections that happen in real time which will improve and strengthen their wellbeing. In real time it is a relief to find a place where we can be accepted and belong as our true and vulnerable self, where we can put down our phones with all the filters we have learned to hide behind. It's long been documented that young people who are involved in religious activities and who have a clear belief system have more positive health outcomes and a better quality of life.

One of the core values of this generation is community and this is exactly what the local youth group provides. In a world where they are constantly connected remotely, there is a greater sense of disconnection than ever before. This is one of the most treasured things about us sending our own kids to youth. We see our kids off their phones and relating in real time. Our leaders and young people are very rarely on their screens when they are together. They are looking one another in the eye, talking, laughing and creating moments that are oxygen to their souls.

Do you understand how important you are? Do you know how grateful so many parents are for you? Can you comprehend the life skills you are imparting to these young people which is setting them up for a life of meaningful connection and relational success?

Just recently as we were packing down the last load of sound equipment, he came to me. A young man who's loved God for such a short while and who has been through more than most. His eyes held mine as the words tumbled out his mouth. *Thank you to you and Cam for what you have done here. If you hadn't, I would have had nobody.* He was me. I was him. Our stories were the same, just separated by the years. I told him. *How could we not?* I said. *How could we not when somebody else did the same for me.* We chatted until we were the last ones there, hearts brimming with gratitude for the friends who became family, the church who became a lifeline. Our life blood.

So please, keep looking up and never stop looking young people in the eye. Inspire them to put their phones down and live in the moment, because when you do, their lives are impacted more than you could know. Keep having the conversations that to you might be mere words, but to them are a line to hold on to, that keeps them afloat and gives them what they cannot find anywhere else.

May it never end...hearts undone on the high school floor

IN CONCLUSION

It was over 20 years ago that a group of students gathered with a great leader, a once in a generation leader with a guitar in a school hall.

It was over 20 years ago that those young hearts were laid bare before God on the high school floor in an Adelaide suburb. Now those same souls have gone on to have families that love Jesus. Some we've lost in the fight. Others have gone on to write songs and lead churches that are changing the world.

Here we are today having come full circle. 20 years on and in another school hall. We began *Public Youth* even before we began the church because young people mean everything to us.

This time it was a new group of young leaders and a guy called Joey with his guitar. We started with nothing and yet with everything we needed, because we understood all the heart lessons we have put before you in these pages.

All those years ago we began, with a handful of kids and the best team of leaders with the biggest hearts we know. It's been simple, yet it's been profound. What God did, 20 years ago, in that leadership team in Russell and Sam's lounge, we can see He's doing again.

We've been digging down and not worrying about building up, teaching our team what true care looks like, sounds like and feels like. It's been about going into the local high school with no other agenda than to love the youth and teaching team, it's why making phone calls still works today. We believe in the power of the small gathering, consistently and often and so we launched *'Squads'* straight away. It's been about making crazy memories at Camp Drewe and having plenty of conversations – the hard kind, but the saving kind too. We've modelled the conversations with our leaders who have then gone on to do the same with our young people.

There's been the highs of seeing our first lot of year 12's graduate, where we turned out in full force to their pre-formals. We look at those photos and smile because we can't believe it's been almost 8 years. But our hearts are so intertwined that we can't remember it any other way.

There's also been the lows of burying a father, wiping tears and staying silent because we had no words. Just sitting together, in the dark.

Though our social media is amazing and creative and we're so proud, it's all been for us... it's our album of memories. It's the way we've told our God story as it's unfolded. But we know that deep down and behind the lens, is a healthy and functional foundation. We've been building according to the crazy. It's not been done before, the blueprint handed directly to us from the heart of God himself.

Most of all, it's been encountering Jesus and right in front of our eyes we're watching God do it again – what He did 20 years ago. Hearts undone. Right there on the high school floor.

And here we sit, on the eve of another story we are about to write, our pen poised on the paper, with great anticipation of what God will do in another new space. In six sleeps we are planting another new work of God, this time in *Public* Brisbane. This time we have Poppy! The out-of-the-box one who bleeds God's call in her veins! She will be the one helping to form what this new season looks like for our *Public* youth in Brisbane. One thing we can tell you for sure is that nothing is for sure. We built one way just over 8 years ago but that does not make it the pattern for this way. One thing is the same though. We begin again in a hall, a sweet white chapel with creaking old wooden floorboards and a thousand secrets seeping in their cracks. The method might be different. The pattern will be unfamiliar. One thing will be the same – hearts undone on the floor as they encounter the love of God.

We know we've just begun. The story of what God will do with our hearts and the hearts of our youth is God's story, for Him to yet tell.

Always remember what God is doing where you are, is another beautiful, original, breath-taking story. It's the beginning of the beginning. Do your story well. Dig deep. Don't waver. Love the one. Don't boast. It's about them, not you. Be yourself. Build according to God's plan. Lead them to the Cross.

It's the beginning of the beginning. Live your story. Tell your story. Nobody is cheering you on louder than we are and perhaps one day, if we ever get to sit down with you, it will be our honour to hear your God story. Collectively, we will see Jesus transform a generation.

May it never end... hearts undone on the high school floor.

ABOUT CAM AND RENEE

Cam and Renee Bennett are the Directors of *Youth Alive*, Australia's largest Christian youth movement.

Directors since 2014, the ministry of *Youth Alive* has reached hundreds of thousands of young people with the gospel of Jesus Christ. As pioneers who create platforms to develop and unlock the next generation, Cam and Renee have founded:

United We Stand - Australia's largest Christian youth outreach, bringing over 30 000 young people together on one night to lift up the name of Jesus

Youth Alive Academy - a leadership college now with locations nationwide, training youth leaders and pastors.

UNIVS - a National movement reaching young adults and universities with the gospel of Jesus Christ

Cam and Renee are greatly trusted and two of the most experienced leaders of youth and young adults in Australia and beyond. They are also the lead pastors of Public Church, based in Gold Coast and Brisbane, Queensland, Australia.